INSTITUTE OF MANAGEMENT AND LABOR RELATIONS SERIES—RUTGERS, THE STATE UNIVERSITY OF NEW JERSEY

Editor: James Chelius

1. *Reflections on the Transformation of Industrial Relations,* edited by James Chelius and James Dworkin. 1990

2. *Profit Sharing and Gain Sharing,* edited by Myron J. Roomkin. 1990

3. *The Mediator Revisited: Profile of a Profession, 1960s and 1985,* by Ruth F. Necheles-Jansyn. 1990

THE MEDIATOR REVISITED

profile of a profession
1960s and 1985

by
Ruth F. Necheles-Jansyn

*Institute of Management and Labor Relations
Series, No. 3*

IMLR Press / Rutgers University
and
The Scarecrow Press, Inc.
Metuchen, N.J., & London, 1990

British Library Cataloguing-in-Publication data available

Library of Congress Cataloging-in-Publication Data

Necheles-Jansyn, Ruth F., 1936-
    The mediator revisited : profile of a profession, 1960s and 1985 /
by Ruth F. Necheles-Jansyn.
        p.   cm. -- (Institute of Management and Labor Relations Se-
ries ; no. 3)
    Includes bibliographical references and index.
    ISBN 0-8108-2351-9 (alk. paper)
    1. Mediation and conciliation, Industrial--United States.   I. Title.
II. Series.
HD5504.A3N43   1990
331.89'142'0973--dc20   90-42215

CONTENTS

Figures and Tables v
Editor's Note vii
Preface ix

1. **Introduction** 1
   Studying mediators, the survey: instrument and administration
2. **The History of Mediation** 9
3. **Portrait of the Labor Mediator** 27
   Introduction, the 1985 mediator,
   changes over a quarter century
4. **The Mediation Career** 43
   Job satisfaction, preparation and
   professionalism
5. **Collective Bargaining Issues** 56
   Introduction, attitudes toward unions
   and the American collective bargaining
   system, conclusions
6. **Mediation and the American Industrial** 69
   Relations System
   Role in the American industrial relations system, the mediator's job
7. **Professional Issues in Mediation** 84
   Status, recognition and other issues,
   mediation strategy and tactics,
   conclusions
8. **Interpreting Observed Differences:** 100
   The Job and the System
   Introduction, job satisfaction, unions
   and collective bargaining, the mediators'
   role in collective bargaining, summary
   and conclusions
9. **Interpreting Observed Differences on** 115
   Professional Issues and Mediation Tactics
   Professional issues, voluntarism and
   dependence, tactics and strategy, summary and conclusions
10. **Conclusions** 132

Appendix A: A Note on Methods 141
Appendix B: The 1985 Survey Instrument 145
Bibliography 181
Index 191

FIGURES AND TABLES

Figures

2-1. Employment, by Sector, 1850-1982   17
3-1. Highest Educational Achievement   28
3-2. 1984 Salary and Income   28
3-3. Age, by Agency   31
3-4. 1984 Salary and Income, by Agency   34
3-5. 1960s Salary and Income, by Agency   36
3-6. Age by Agency, 1960s and 1985   37
4-1. Job Satisfaction, by Years at Agency,
     1985   44
4-2. Future Career Plans, 1960s and 1985   46
4-3. Willingness to Accept Job Related Risks,
     by Agency, 1960s and 1985   49
5-1. Attitudes Toward Unions, by Agency and
     by Type of Cases   61
7-1. Should Follow Case if Site Changes, by
     Agency and Type of Cases   86
7-2. Should Keep Clients, by Agency and Type
     of Cases   87
8-1. Education and Age   103
8-2. Career Plans, by Age   106
8-3. Unions Hinder Superior Workers, by
     Agency, Type of Cases and Past Union
     Employment   110
9-1. Retaining Clientele, by Agency   116
9-2. Dual Mediation Satisfies Parties, by
     Agency; Dual Mediation Unsatisfactory
     for Mediators, by Agency   118

Tables

1-1. Response, by Region   6
3-1. Type of Cases Normally Handled, by Agency   34
4-1. Job Satisfaction by Salary Satisfaction:
     1985   47
4-2. Job Stress: Authority and Responsibility   50
4-3. Job Stress, by Agency, 1960s and 1985   51
5-1. Attitudes Toward Unions, by FMCS Region   59
5-2. Scope of Bargaining: Managerial Rights   63
6-1. Mediator Responsibility, by Agency   73
6-2. Attitudes Toward Compulsory Arbitration,
     by Agency   77
7-1. When Prefer to Enter, 1960s and 1985   93
7-2. Settlement Tactics, by Agency   94
8-1. Job Satisfaction, by Agency: Controlling
     for Mediator Experience and for Satis-
     factory Client Relationships   102
9-1. When Enter in Theory, by Agency: Con-
     trolling for No Management Experience   123

EDITOR'S NOTE

THE INSTITUTE OF MANAGEMENT AND LABOR RELATIONS of Rutgers University, The State University of New Jersey, was founded by the state legislature with a mandate to educate labor, management, and the public on matters concerning the employment relationship. With this series, it is our intention to further this goal by publishing books that will make a significant contribution to communicating the results of research on various aspects of industrial relations, human resource management, and employment policy.

JAMES CHELIUS
Series Editor
Institute of Management
   and Labor Relations
Rutgers University

PREFACE

The idea of replicating its quarter-century-old study of mediator backgrounds, self-image and attitudes was conceived by the Rutgers Institute of Management and Labor Relations (IMLR) early in the 1980s. Although other projects prevented him from conducting the research himself, Professor William M. Weinberg convinced me that it was a worthwhile undertaking, and he has worked closely with me through all of its phases.

Three institutions -- Rutgers, the Association of Labor Relations Agencies (ALRA) and the Federal Mediation and Conciliation Service (FMCS) -- have supported my work. Rutgers provided clerical, computer and photocopying facilities while ALRA and FMCS duplicated and distributed the questionnaires. In addition, a sabbatical leave from Long Island University provided the time necessary for analyzing data and reporting results.

In addition to the assistance, advice and encouragement offered by Dr. Weinberg, Jeffery Tener, the executive secretary of ALRA, and Paul Yager, the former FMCS North East Regional Director, I benefited greatly from the programming expertise of Batiste Borio. My husband, Leon R. Jansyn, provided moral support and helpful hints concerning statistical methods.

In acknowledging assistance, however, credit really should be given first to the mediators who took the time to respond, and particularly to those who bothered to comment on individual items. Without their cooperation, this study would not have been possible.

December 1987   Ruth F. Necheles-Jansyn
                                 Long Island University,
                                 Brooklyn Campus

CHAPTER I.   INTRODUCTION

Studying Mediators

By the late 1950s the practice of labor mediation had matured and the use of agency staff to assist in the resolution of industrial disputes had become sufficiently widespread that mediators and scholars alike perceived the need to study the profession seriously. Initiative was taken by the Association of State Mediation Agencies (ASMA), the name by which the Association of Labor Relations Agencies (or ALRA) was then known. It, in cooperation with the New York State Board of Mediation and the Cornell School of Industrial and Labor Relations (ILR), sponsored two important research projects. Both projects were also supported by the Office of Naval Research.

The first study, undertaken by Ann Douglas, consisted of observing and analyzing data on live labor mediations. Her Industrial Peacemaking (1962) contains what are still the most complete and useful transcripts of labor negotiations ever compiled.

The second scholar whose investigations were jointly sponsored was Henry Landsberger.[1] His work differed from that undertaken by Douglas in that he was concerned with developing psychological tests capable of screening potential mediators. Although he isolated three major traits which, according to him, a mediator should possess, he never found one or more tests which successfully selected among candidates and predicted their ability.

Douglas' and Landsberger's investigations covered only a limited number of mediators and a narrow geographic region. Moreover, they included only staff employed by state agencies. Other studies conducted in the late 1950s suffered from the same limitations. It was not until the early 1960s, when the Rutgers Institute of Management and Labor Relations (the IMLR) conducted surveys of American and Canadian state, provincial and federal mediators, that it became possible to look at the profession as a whole.

1

Based on the results of the Rutgers surveys,
in the early 1960s researchers concluded that
significant differences existed between mediators
employed by state agencies and by the Federal
Mediation and Conciliation Service (the FMCS).
The most significant difference that they
discovered was that, in general, federal mediators
tended to favor more active strategies than did
their state colleagues; as one observer noted,
the FMCS appeared more anxious to assist clients
while state mediators preferred to wait until a
crisis had developed.

By the early 1980s, some observers argued
that state mediators had become more intervention-
ist than their federal colleagues. Several writers
attributed the increasing difference between state
and federal mediators as to when they should intervene in disputes to the difference in the types
of cases that they normally handled; in the 1980s
many state agencies concentrated on public sector
cases while FMCS mediators continued to hear private sector disputes.[2] For this reason it was
assumed that differences between state and federal
mediators probably had probably increased since
the Rutgers surveys were completed in the mid-
1960s.

The growth of public sector collective bargaining was not the only change that had taken
place in the American industrial relations system
which might have affected mediator attitudes.
Even within the private sector, inflationary
trends of the 1970s coupled with the decline in
such heavily unionized industries as automotive,
coal and steel had transformed the American economy and had altered the environment in which
collective bargaining took place. The proportion
of the labor force that belonged to employee
organizations declined; reportedly, American public opinion became less favorable toward unions.

It would be interesting to measure the extent
to which these environmental changes influenced
the attitudes of mediators employed full-time by
federal and state agencies toward the American
industrial relations system and toward their profession. Fortunately, the Rutgers surveys provide
a yardstick for measuring change.[3] The first,
dating from 1962, was developed and administered

in cooperation with what by then had come to be
known as the Association of Labor Mediation
Agencies (ALMA). It investigated the characteristics and attitudes of mediators employed by the
state and provincial agencies that belonged to
ALMA. Two years later IMLR gained the cooperation
of the FMCS in conducting a similar study of
federal mediators.

The timing of the original Rutgers surveys
was fortunate because they were administered only
shortly before public sector collective bargaining
began to proliferate, first at the state and then
at the federal level. The American economy, as
yet unaffected by the Vietnam War and by cooperative action among the petroleum exporting coun-
tries, gave no grounds for concern or doubt. The
survey results, therefore, provide an excellent
basis upon which the impact on the profession of
external and internal change can be measured.

The two 1960s surveys revealed interesting
similarities and differences between federal and
state mediators. Both groups had almost identical
amounts of labor relations and collective bargaining experience; most mediators had belonged to
unions and over one-half had held a paid union
position. But federal mediators were older than
their state colleagues. In the early 1960s the
proportion of mediators with under three years of
experience in both state and federal agencies had
declined in comparison with their more senior colleagues. A greater percentage of state mediators
came from lower social origins than did the FMCS
staff. On the whole, all mediators were satisfied
with their jobs and believed that they had done as
well or better than they had expected. Unsurprisingly, FMCS staff were more satisfied with their
salaries. State mediators reported more job related stresses and hoped to find better jobs outside their present agency.

Twenty-five years ago all agency mediators
accepted the American industrial relations system
and believed that unions had made positive contri-
butions to modern life. While they agreed that
mediation contributed significantly to maintaining
industrial peace, they differed on questions of
timing and strategy. Federal mediators wished to
enter disputes earlier than their state colleagues

even though they actually entered at roughly the
same stage of negotiations as did their state
colleagues. A somewhat larger number of FMCS than
state mediators selected responses favoring more
active intervention in disputes.

The Survey: Instrument and Administration

In order to see how the mediators' backgrounds and attitudes had changed over the quarter
century that had elapsed since the original survey
was conducted, the survey instrument should be
kept as close to the original as possible. Nonetheless, the 1960s questionnaires could not simply
be duplicated because there were significant differences between the 1962 state and the 1964 FMCS
forms. Moreover, a few of the questions no longer
were important and the wording of several lacked
precision. New questions were needed in order to
measure the effect on mediator attitudes of public
sector and health care collective bargaining as
well as changed economic conditions. Needless to
say, the 1960s salary ranges had to be revised
completely; it was impossible to make them comparable to 1985 wage levels.

Some changes caused confusion. For example,
the question designed to measure family social
status was changed to ask for "parents'" rather
than "father's occupation." The answers proved
very difficult to score; did multiple responses
(8% of the total) indicate "moonlighting" or did
they reflect two-earner families? Several respondents checked three or more categories.

Other changes that should have been made were
not. Thus, through an oversight, the question
concerning educational levels asked only about the
father's education. As one respondent pointed
out, "There is a very different mix of family
relationships today, including single heads of
households, stepfathers or stepmothers and other
arrangements." And, she asserted, "statistics
reveal that more women are receiving higher degrees than men."[4] There is room for doubt,
therefore, concerning responses to this question.
Other problems with phrasing will be discussed in
the text below.

The revised questionnaires were mailed in
February 1985. The FMCS director, Kay McMurray,

added a cover letter to the federal form, and his
agency distributed the questionnaire to its staff.
ALRA distributed the state/provincial form to its
member agencies.

ALRA sent an additional questionnaire to
agency heads asking about current job titles,
salary ranges and hiring requirements, and whether
mediator positions were covered by civil service.
It also asked how many applications had been received during the previous year, how many vacancies had been filled, and how many were anticipated for the following year (1985).

Eighteen of the twenty United States agency
heads responded to the separate questionnaire as
did two of the four Canadian directors. They reported from one to six mediator titles, and positions in fourteen of the twenty responding agencies were covered by civil service. Mediation was
an attractive field; agencies reported anywhere
from 300 to one application to fill a very few
vacancies (Puerto Rico reported the most new positions -- eight -- while nine agencies hired no
mediators in 1984). Only eight agencies anticipated adding staff in 1985. As might be expected,
salary levels varied considerably among the responding state agencies. The lowest scale, as reported by administrators, ranged from $12,000 to
$23,000 per year while the highest went from
$34,000 to $55,000.[5] The narrowest range was
$7,000 and the largest was $25,000 (both agencies
employed five mediators).

The questionnaires were returned within a
short period of time, and the responses were coded
in Spring 1985. (The methods used are discussed
below in Appendix A.) The overall response rate
was 56%. FMCS staff were the more enthusiastic
participants; 62% of them returned their questionnaires. Fifty-eight percent of the United States
state mediators responded while only 20% of their
Canadian colleagues did so. Evidently many of the
latter found the questionnaire irrelevant or
unsuited to their particular circumstances. Consequently, their answers were not used in the
federal/state comparisons, although they were
included in other computations.

The largest proportion of the FMCS responses came from the Central Region, and 70% of the midwestern state mediators returned their questionnaires as compared with 48% of the western state mediators.[6]   Only two southern state agencies employing one or two mediators respectively (North Carolina and Arkansas) belong to ALRA and hence participated in the survey (see Table 1 below). The results, therefore, are slightly skewed toward the older, industrialized areas.

TABLE 1. Response by Region

	FMCS			State		
	mailed	returned	%	mailed	returned	%
Total	235	146	62%	179	104	58%
By region:						
Eastern	34			72	36	50
Southern	34			3	2	66
Central	50			57	40	70
Western	26			42	20	48
National	2					
Puerto Rico				5	5	100
Canada				50	10	20
unidentified					1	

About one-fifth of the participants commented at the end of the questionnaire about the survey instrument, professional issues, and/or government policies.   Federal mediators were more likely to make any comment at all than were their colleagues in state agencies, and they were more likely to discuss government policies. State mediators, for their part, were slightly more likely to remark on professional issues (6% as compared with 5.5% of the comments made by FMCS mediators).   Interestingly enough, even though state mediators handled almost all of the public sector cases, the respondents who dealt with public sector clients were as likely to comment on the questionnaire as were those who handled private sector cases. Evidently the difference in willingness to comment depended more on agency affiliation than on type of clients.

Although they made fewer comments in the space provided at the end of the questionnaire, more state than federal respondents remarked on individual questions as they filled out the form, and a few provided running commentaries on the issues throughout the questionnaire. Most critical statements concerned specific phraseology, although some participants pointed to areas that either had been neglected or should have been investigated more thoroughly. In general, the participants' comments focused on recent developments in mediation, and respondents demonstrated the greatest uncertainty concerning new issues or problems. Most remarks were favorable, although a few, such as, "amateurish questions on the process," counterbalance statements from those who found the survey "in general [to be] just shy of excellent."

Mediators apparently were no longer as enthusiastic about studying themselves as they had been a quarter of a century before. Some of them, indeed, considered themselves to be "studied out." Nonetheless, their responses indicated a continuing concern about professional questions as well as a growing sophistication about the issues.

As anticipated, mediators changed between the 1960s and 1985. Whether this change was as great as had been assumed and whether it can be attributed either to the growth of public sector collective bargaining or to the maturation of agency mediators will be investigated in detail below. First, however, the political, legal and economic context in which agency mediation developed will be described briefly.

NOTES

1. Landsberger's research was reported in several journals between 1955 and 1962; see bibliography.

2. William H. Weinberg, "Bureaucratic Expediency and the Ethics of Mediation," prepared for presentation to the Association of Labor Relations Agencies, Aug. 15, 1967, San Francisco, and Deborah Kolb, The Mediators (Cambridge, Mass.: Massachusetts Institute of Technology Press, 1983).

3. Reported in Allen Weisenfeld, "Profile of a Labor Mediator," Labor Law Journal, Oct. 1962, pp. 864-73; Monroe Berkowitz, Bernard Goldstein and Bernard P. Indik, "The State Mediator: Background, Self-Image and Attitudes," Industrial and Labor Relations Review, 17 (Jan. 1964); and Indik et. al., The Mediator: Background, Self-Image, and Attitudes (New Brunswick, N.J.: Institute of Labor and Management Relations, Rutgers, 1966).

4. Jean McKee, letter March 13, 1985. Another mediator appended a lengthy comment to the same effect.

5. Averages are given in Chapter 3.

6. Response rates for FMCS regions cannot be calculated because it is not known how many questionnaires were sent to each office.

CHAPTER 2.   THE HISTORY OF MEDIATION

Mediation is a venerable occupation. Yet it often is confused with arbitration, and until recently the term was used interchangeably with arbitration, conciliation and collective bargaining. A more precise definition developed as what we now call collective bargaining spread and the various methods of third party dispute resolution became increasingly common.

In the early years of American history, religious leaders helped resolve disputes between workers and employers, settlers and governors. When, during the later part of the nineteenth century, industrial disputes increased in frequency and intensity, a few states authorized public agencies to appoint ad hoc tribunals, or arbitration boards, to assist in settling industrial conflicts.

Maryland was the first to act in 1879, one year after a violent railroad strike, and New Jersey followed shortly thereafter. Arbitration statutes were passed in Pennsylvania and Ohio during the early 1880s, and in 1886, a year which saw both the Haymarket Riot and the organization of the American Federation of Labor, New York and Massachusetts established permanent state mediation agencies. Other states passed similar legislation and by 1913 thirty-two states authorized third-party assistance in resolving industrial conflict. Nonetheless, significant mediation activity occurred in only four states, Massachusetts, New York, Ohio and Illinois.

Some of the state agencies were short lived because the attitudes necessary for successful mediation were lacking; neither side was willing to settle differences through voluntary agreement. Managements were unwilling to recognize the workers' right to organize, while unions that had sufficient economic power to force recognition were conflict-oriented and were not interested in establishing a working relationship with employers. But few unions had such power, and state agencies had insufficient authority to deal with recognitional issues. Without enabling legisla-

9

tion, which most states failed to enact until the
1930s, mediation proved ineffectual. As the New
York State Board of Mediation and Arbitration observed:

> When the employer recognizes the indis-
> putable fact that combinations of working-
> men exist, and also their right to demand
> fair compensation for services, and other
> conditions, it is not difficult for the
> Board to bring representatives of the two
> parties together and accomplish an adjust-
> ment of their differences. When employers
> refuse to recognize organized workingmen
> and will treat with them only as indivi-
> duals, thus effacing the trade organiza-
> tion, there remains substantially but one
> party to the case, viz., the employer;
> hence little opportunity for arbitration.[2]

At the federal level, mediation institutions
developed first in the most troubled area, the
railroad industry. In 1898 the Erdman Act established the Railway Labor Board with power to investigate industrial disputes and to recommend
settlement terms. Unions, which were awarded legal recognition by this statute, were required to
post notice and to submit to mediation or arbitration before engaging in a strike. Between 1906
and 1913 the Erdman Act successfully avoided all
but one serious disruption of railway service.
But by 1913 the four part-time mediators desig-
nated by the act proved unable to meet the demand
for their services, and Congress created a Board
of Mediation and Conciliation within the newly
established Department of Labor.

Although the Board of Mediation and Conciliation employed four full-time mediators, this
staff proved inadequate as, during the 1920s,
increasing competition from the automobile led to
hightened labor-management tensions. Ultimately,
the carriers and the railroad unions created their
own dispute settlement procedures which Congress
enacted into law in the 1926 Railway Labor Act.
This law established a federal mediation agency
which was separate from the Department of Labor
and which became known as the National Mediation
Board.[3]

The Labor Department's Board of Mediation and Conciliation assisted in settling disputes in industries other than railways. In 1917 it was reorganized as the United States Conciliation Service (USCS) and was allotted a staff of thirteen and a budget of $50,000. Throughout World War I the USCS and the War Labor Board, in accordance with a public policy designed to maintain a balance between unions and employers, played an active role in ensuring industrial peace. Existing unions were given a protection which they had not possessed previously, and their membership nearly doubled, but they were forbidden to demand a closed shop in workplaces where it had not existed previously.

Immediately following World War I public opinion, influenced by the "Red hysteria" of 1919-20, turned against organized labor. By 1923 union membership had declined from its 1920 peak of 5 million to approximately 3.6 million. Despite industrial prosperity during the later 1920s, unions failed to recover, and in 1929 total membership was 3.4 million, the lowest it had been since 1917.

By 1933 unions numbered fewer than three million members. Public policy toward unions changed; injunctions against union activities were restricted by the Norris-LaGuardia Act, and first the National Industrial Recovery Act and then the Wagner Act provided positive protection for the right to organize and to bargain collectively. The National Labor Board of 1933 was authorized to settle by mediation, conciliation or arbitration any controversy which threatened the purposes of the NRA. Recognition remained the stumbling block, and the Board lacked the power to enforce its decisions. Recognition strikes continued, and in 1935 Congress passed the Wagner Act, Section 1 of which declared:

> The denial by employers of the right of employees to organize and the refusal by employers to accept the procedure of collective bargaining lead to strikes and other forms of industrial strife or unrest, which have the intent or the necessary effect of burdening or obstructing commerce. . . .

> Experience has proved that protection by
> law of the right of employees to organize
> and bargain collectively safeguards com-
> merce from injury, impairment, or inter-
> ruption, and promotes the flow of commerce
> by removing certain recognized sources of
> industrial strife and unrest, by encourag-
> ing practices fundamental to the friendly
> adjustment of industrial disputes arising
> out of differences as to wages, hours or
> other working conditions, and by restoring
> equality of bargaining power between em-
> ployers and employees.

Congress established the National Labor Relations
Board (NLRB) as a permanent, independent agency
with authority to administer the act, but its jurisdiction was limited to unfair labor practices
and to representational conflicts.

Following Supreme Court confirmation of the
constitutionality of the Wagner Act in 1937, attitudes toward dispute settlement began to change.
Although recognitional controversies remained
bitter, the NLRB provided machinery for their
resolution and, in theory at least, they no longer
were settled by collective bargaining and strikes.
Negotiations between employers and employee organizations now focused on substantive contractual
issues which the parties were more willing to submit to third-party resolution.

Under the changed environment created by the
NLRA, the USCS could no longer meet the demand for
its services, and some raised doubts concerning
the competence of its staff. More important,
overcen tralized procedures led to considerable
delays in responding to disputes, and several
industrialized states and cities either
refurbished existing dispute settlement agencies
or established new ones. Among the cities, Tol-
edo's service served as model for the agencies
created in 1937 or shortly thereafter in
Cincinnati, Denver, Newark, New York, Philadelphia
and Sheboygan. But municipal agencies proved too
limited, and by 1941 such states as Connecticut,
Massachusetts, Michigan, New Jersey, New York,
Pennsylvania and Wisconsin had created full
mediation services.[4]

Peaceful resolution of industrial disputes appeared even more important as war spread in Europe and the Far East and the international demand for American industrial products increased. In March 1941, even before the United States entered the conflict, President Roosevelt established a National Defense Mediation Board. But this agency foundered on the rock that destroyed several state mediation boards, the union shop issue.[5]

Following Pearl Harbor, the AFL, CIO, National Association of Manufacturers and the United States Chamber of Commerce adopted an informal no-strike, no-lockout policy which was administered by a newly-created National War Labor Board. Tripartite regional labor boards, some of whose members were recruited from state and municipal mediation agencies, ensured cooperation between federal and local boards.

With some notable exceptions, war-time labor-management relations were harmonious. The Secretary of Labor certified disputes to the War Labor Board, which refused to act unless parties could prove that they had first tried mediation. The board's "maintenance of membership" policy avoided the thorny union shop problem and was instrumental in maintaining labor peace.

Difficulties developed as consumer prices continued to rise even while the War Labor Board attempted to restrict wage increases to fifteen percent above the January 1941 level. A series of work stoppages in spring 1943, the most dramatic of which briefly closed the coal mines, brought agitation for anti-strike legislation to a head, and in June Congress passed the Smith-Connally Act over a presidential veto. This law required parties to file notices with the USCS thirty days before striking a defense industry and it authorized the NLRB to conduct a strike vote among union members if the dispute was not settled during the so-called "cooling off period." Instigating or aiding a strike became a criminal offense.

The Smith-Connally Act established the first mandatory mediation procedures in American labor law, and it gave mediators a more active role because they now had the power to decide when to

enter a dispute. The hostile response of several
state agencies to the provision that appeared to
give the USCS priority in settling disputes led
the War Labor Board to accept certification by any
agency as fulfilling statutory requirements.[6]

By the end of the war, the federal conciliation service employed two hundred and fifty mediators in regional offices located in the major industrial centers. Mediation, as a means of settling industrial disputes, had been dramatized
during the war, and it now became an integral part
of the American industrial relations system.

The prospect of world peace revived prewar
questions concerning national labor policy. During the last year of the war the number of strikes
increased sharply, and those industrialists and
Congressmen who had never approved of the Wagner
Act now attacked the law on three grounds: that it
vested too much authority in federal hands, that
it led to federal interference with management
rights, and that it violated the principle of
voluntary association by infringing on the workers' right not to join unions. State mediation
agencies, fearing that the wartime extension of
federal jurisdiction over local labor disputes
would continue, also lobbied for amendments to the
Wagner Act which would clarify their role.

The Taft-Hartley Act of 1947 embodied the in-
tentions of those who wanted to weaken, as well as
those who only wished to restrict, the USCS's jurisdiction. This law made several significant
changes in national labor policy affecting dispute
settlement. Under it, the federal mediation
agency (renamed the Federal Mediation and Conciliation Service, or the FMCS) became a statutory
body independent of the Department of Labor.
Newly created emergency procedures mandated recourse to this agency. But the law recognized
state agencies in that it instructed the federal
service to mediate disputes with a substantial impact on interstate commerce and to refrain from
intervening in those which had only a "minor" impact. The notification clause was amended to require parties to inform all mediation agencies,
state as well as federal, thirty days before ter-
minating or revising a contract. Thus state
agencies, where they existed, were to be kept in-

formed of potential conflict and could offer their services.

Although Congress revised the national labor law again in 1957, the Landrum-Griffin Act made no further changes in the mediation system which had developed in response to the Taft-Hartley amendments. The system devised in 1947, sometimes referred to as the NLRA system (because, technically, the later labor laws merely amended the Wagner Act), thus continued to serve as the legal context for industrial relations in the United States.

Between 1945 and 1947 members of the various state mediation agencies met in order to coordinate their attempts to limit federal intervention in local disputes. Once the FMCS was established, state mediation officials met with the officers of the new agency in order to work out jurisdictional guidelines. Over the next decade, friction between the federal and the state agencies receded into the background.

In part, tension between federal and state mediators had arisen out of a mutual lack of respect. In the postwar years, mediators became concerned with improving their reputation and self-image through cooperative action, in particular, through membership in professional organizations. Although mediators participated in the activities of the International Association of Government Labor Officials and the Industrial Relations Research Association (IRRA), state mediators wanted an organization that focused on problems in dispute resolution and was free of what they considered to be the political influence of state and federal labor department officials. In 1952 they organized the Association of State Mediation Agencies (ASMA), which became an active force in formulating and promulgating professional standards.[7]

From the first, ASMA sponsored research. Although its members tended to be pragmatic and "atheoretical," they were interested in collecting data about mediation and exchanging ideas about training and recruitment. Their interest in recruitment stemmed from three factors: increased concern about professionalization, the retirement of the first generation of mediators, who had

learned their trade in the war labor boards, and
the expansion of mediation services to meet the
increasing demands of the 1960s and 1970s.

Because of the mediators' concern with recruitment, early ASMA programs frequently discussed training techniques. Nonetheless, the nature
of American federalism and jurisdictional differences among the various agencies prevented the establishment of uniform standards for mediators. A
tentative step in this direction occurred in 1964
when a joint committee of ASMA and FMCS devised a
code of professional conduct which condemned many
of the federal practices that the state agencies
had long since criticized.

In 1972 ASMA became the Association of Labor
Mediation Agencies (ALMA) and admitted the FMCS
and the Canadian national service to membership.
Five years later it once again changed its name to
Association of Labor Relations Agencies (ALRA),
signaling its interest in attracting such purely
adjudication agencies as the NLRB to membership.
Although at one time it considered accepting individual memberships, it declined to do so, and membership remained limited to agencies.

In the meantime, in 1973, the FMCS was instrumental in establishing a new organization, the
Society of Professionals in Dispute Resolution, or
SPIDR, over which it continued to exert a strong
influence. Unlike ALRA, SPIDR accepted individual
members, some of whom resolved disputes in such
diverse areas as divorce, commerce and international relations, as well as in industrial
relations.

For a time ALRA and SPIDR co-sponsored projects, but cooperation between the two societies
ceased after 1977. By 1985 ALRA had become more
active in pursuing research projects, particularly
those which concerned labor-management issues. In
addition, the older organization, IRRA, encouraged serious research on these topics.

These organizations, as well as several
others which attracted smaller groups within the
mediation profession, were instrumental in helping
mediators to recognize and adjust to the new
issues created by changes in the American economy

and the consequent transformation of the American
labor force.[8]

These changes were dramatic. As Figure 1
shows, by the early 1960s the proportion of
workers employed in the goods-producing sector had
begun to decline while employment in service industries had increased significantly. The number
of state and local government employees had also
grown rapidly from 11.9% of the work force in 1959
to 17.1% in 1984.[9]

These shifts significantly affected the labor
movement. As employment declined in such highly
organized industries as steel, automobiles and
coal, the proportion of the total labor force
represented by unions fell rapidly from 25.5%
during the peak year, 1953, to 20.7% in 1984.[10]

FIGURE 1. Employment by Sector: 1850-1982

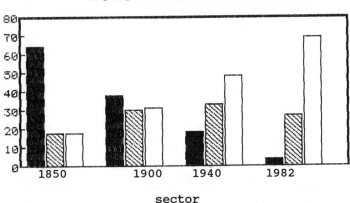

sector
■ agricultural   ▨ goods   ☐ services

Michael Urquhart, "The Employment Shift to Services: Where Did It Come From?" Monthly Labor
Review, April 1984, p. 16.

The areas in which employment was expanding
in the early 1980s, the service, professional and

health-care sectors, proved difficult to organize
despite early optimism. The only sector in which
significant unionization has taken place was the
public sector, where membership rose from 1.3% in
1956, the first year for which figures were available, to 6.1% in 1984.

Collective bargaining developed slowly in
such service industries as fast food that employed
unskilled, part-time, young and/or minority workers. While the stormy history of teamster and
migrant worker organization provided some prece-
dents, they were ones that most employers preferred to avoid.

Collective bargaining among salaried professionals had better potential for growth, although it, too, developed unevenly. The Taft-
Hartley Act specifically authorized professionals
to form unions, but they were slow to take advantage of their opportunity.

The only professional group that actively
pursued collective bargaining consisted of faculty
in institutions of higher learning, where for a
decade organization spread rapidly. After 1980,
however, faculty organization was crippled by the
Supreme Court's <u>Yeshiva</u> decision, which declared
at least some academicians to be managerial.
Thereafter unionization continued to expand, but
at a more modest rate. Faculty efforts were encouraged by the Supreme Court's 1986 refusal to
review a federal circuit court's ruling that
sanctioned collective bargaining at Cooper Union
in New York City. Still, by 1987, faculty at only
five percent of the private institutions of higher
education were organized, while 61% percent of the
nation's public campuses were unionized.[11]

Unionization among public sector and health
care employees was slower to develop than among
academicians and it, too, remains controversial.
The 1974 amendments to the NLRA extended the NLRB's
jurisdiction over private health care facilities,
while the impetus for public employee organization
came in January 1962 when President Kennedy's
Executive Order 10988 permitted limited collective
bargaining in federal employment. This permission
was broadened by President Nixon, and it became
part of statutory law through the 1978 Civil

Service Reform Act.

For the most part, state legislation lagged behind federal action. Only Wisconsin had a public sector bargaining law before 1962, while other industrialized states passed enabling legislation in the following years. Thereafter membership in public service labor organizations spread rapidly among state and local employees.[12]

With the growth of public sector collective bargaining came an informal division of labor between state and federal mediators. The state agencies no longer contested FMCS jurisdiction over private sector cases and disputes involving federal employees. On the other hand, state agencies, where they existed, concentrated on state and local public sector cases.[13]

For a time, FMCS exercised its jurisdiction cautiously. Although President Nixon's 1970 Executive Order 11491 mandated FMCS assistance in federal labor disputes, at first the Service intervened only when asked and when such intervention did not deprive the private sector of mediation services. Its policy toward state and local public sector disputes was similar.

In 1973 a new FMCS director, W. J. Usery, announced that henceforth the Service would treat state and local disputes in the same way as private sector conflicts. Three years later Herbert Fishgold, FMCS general counsel, announced the expansion of the Service's role in the public sector on the grounds that to ignore "the demanding collective bargaining situations in this area will result in an unstable labor relations climate throughout the nation."[14] He reassured his readers that the FMCS would respect the jurisdiction of existing mediation agencies and indeed would help to develop state facilities.

During the late 1960s and early 1970s associations representing public employees and public school teachers lobbied for federal legislation which either would bring state and local public employees under NLRA jurisdiction or would establish a separate federal commission to regulate state and local employee relations. Although appropriate legislation was introduced between

1970 and 1977,[15] the movement for national regulation was terminated by the Supreme Court's 1976
National League of Cities v. Usery decision.   In
it the court ruled that congressional extension of
the Fair Labor Standards Act to state and local
employees violated the doctrine of intergovern-
mental immunity.

During the Carter administration, various
organizations circulated model state public employee relations bills, while the National Education Association vainly searched for a legislative
formula that would circumvent Tenth Amendment restrictions.   Ronald Reagan's 1980 victory brought
such efforts to an end, and, even though in February 1985 the Supreme Court overruled National
League of Cities on the issue of applying the Fair
Labor Standards Act to state and local governments, public employee organizations did not re-
introduce regulatory legislation.[16]

Opposition to the growth of public sector
collective bargaining surfaced periodically.   In
1976 the Public Service Research Council reported
that public employee bargaining laws led to more
rather than fewer strikes.   The mood of the 1978
Annual School Boards Association Convention was
strongly against government employee collective
bargaining.[17]

By early 1978 criticism of public employee
collective bargaining had spread beyond traditional anti-union camps.   In July 1980 the Government Accounting Office urged the FMCS to cease intervening in state and local public employee disputes because, it claimed, such involvement was of
"questionable legality."   The agency insisted that
the FMCS had failed to cooperate with state mediation services and was meddling in disputes that
did not pose substantial threats to interstate
commerce.   Public employee unions came to the Service's defense, emphasizing the important role
that it played in those states where the mediation
agency was under the governor's direct control.[18]
Local officials also praised the FMCS's work.

Despite such testimonials to its value, the
FMCS suffered from pressure to reduce the federal
budget, and in 1982 the number of regional offices
was halved, physical facilities were cut, and the

support staff was reduced by twenty percent over a period of a few years. Announcing these econo- mies, the new director (Kay McMurray) said that thereafter the federal service would turn to research, study, consultation and analysis rather than direct intervention in labor-management negotiations "in the absence of a compelling national interest."[19]

State mediation agencies were not as directly affected by anti-union sentiment, but they suf- fered even more from budget reductions which di- minished funds available both to their clients and to themselves. Since 1980, except in states which had only recently enacted public bargaining laws and/or created labor relations or mediation agen- cies, there probably was a slight contraction in the demand for their services.

By 1985 some form of mediation services were offered by thirty-five states as well as by Puerto Rico and the Virgin Islands. Of these, in two states such services were offered by departments of labor rather than through separate mediation agencies. The number of full-time state mediators remained small; in 1980 only twelve states em- ployed more than five, and the largest number was twenty.[20]

A precise breakdown of the types of cases handled is impossible to achieve, but scattered data from states with the most active mediation agencies indicates that their work tended to fall largely in the public sector, while 92 of the 99 state mediators who responded to the survey, which will be discussed below, reported that more than half of their cases consisted of public sector disputes.

The mediator's environment changed dramati- cally in the period between the two surveys. Dur- ing this time, mediators were buffeted by the labor market shift away from traditionally organ- ized industries to the more complex and difficult areas of service, health care and public employ- ment. Thus, faced with several new issues, media- tors have had to rethink their attitudes toward themselves, the work that they do, and the en- vironment in which they function. Some of their traditional techniques have required readjustment.

Moreover, after the late 1970s budget constraints became an increasing problem for such publicly funded agencies as the FMCS and state mediation boards.

Thus the mediator of the mid-1980s, when compared with his predecessor of the early 1960s, was less concerned with preserving his jurisdiction from a rival agency. On the other hand, he had a noticeably different clientele and confronted a different set of problems both in servicing his clients and in preserving his career. The following chapters will show the influence that these changes had on the recruitment of mediators, their self-image and their attitudes toward a variety of professional issues.

1. For the history of dispute resolution see: Berkowitz, et. al., "The State Mediator"; Foster Rhea Dulles and Melvyn Dubofsky, Labor in America: A History, 4th ed. (Arlington Heights, Ill.: Harlan Davidson Inc., 1984); Indik, et. al., The Mediator; Kolb The Mediators; Julius Manson, "Mediators as Arbitrators" in New Vistas in Mediation, Proceedings of the Fourth Annual Conference, Association of State Mediation Agencies, Ithaca, New York, June 27-29, 1955, reprinted from Labor Law Journal, Aug. 1955, pp. 587-601; Harry A. Millis and Emily Clark Brown, From the Wagner Act to Taft Hartley: A Study of National Labor Policy and Labor Relations; Charles M. Rehmus, (ed.), The Railway Labor Act at Fifty (Washington, D.C.: U.S. Government Printing Office, 1938); Joseph P. Schuck, "History of Dispute Resolution," in Selected Proceedings of the Twenty-Fifth Annual Conference of the Association of Labor Mediation Agencies (August 14-20, 1976), Ottawa, Canada (n.p., ALMA,, n.d.), pp. 95-99; William M. Weinberg, "An Administrative History of the New Jersey State Board of Mediation," (unpubl. Ph.D. dis., University of Pennsylvania, 1964), pp. 7-11 and his "Impasse Procedures," Arnold Zack and WMW, Resource Manual for Impasse Procedures in Public School Negotiations (New Brunswick, N.J.: Rutgers, IMLR, 1976); Weisenfeld, Mediation; Edwin E. Witte, Historical Survey of Labor Arbitration (Philadelphia: University of Pennsylvania Press, 1952); Leo Wolman, Ebb and Flow in Trade Unionism (New York: National Bureau of Economic Research, 1936).

2. NYSBMA, Seventh Annual Report (1893), cited in Manson, p. 596, n. 53.

3. For the Railway Labor Act, in addition to sources cited in note 1: Administration of The Railway Labor Act by the National Mediation Board, 1934-1970 (Washington, D.C.: U.S. Government Printing Office, [1970]); Walter E. Oberer, Kurt L. Hanslowe and Jerry R. Andersen, Cases and Materials on Labor Law: Collective Bargaining in a Free Society, American Casebook Series, 2nd ed., (St. Paul, Minn.: West Publishing Co., 1979); and W. H. Spencer, The National

Railroad Adjustment Board (Chicago: University of Chicago Press, 1938).

4. Weinberg's several writings on the history of mediation in bibliography; Allan Weisenfeld, Mediation and the Development of Industrial Relations in New Jersey (Newark, N.J.: NJ State Board of Mediation, 1966).

5. Millis-Brown, p. 296.

6. Weinberg, "Bureaucratic Expediency," pp. 22-24 and "Mediators: 25 Years Ago and Today," in Bringing the Dispute Resolution Community Together, 1985 Proceedings, 13th International Conference, October 27-30, 1985, Boston, Massachusetts, Society of Professionals in Dispute Resolution, (Washington, D.C.: SPIDR, 1986), pp. 75-85.

7. Weinberg, "Mediators," p. 4.

8. Thirty-five percent of the respondents to the 1985 survey of mediators said that they belonged to IRRA (although they failed to distinguish between membership in national or local IRRA units) and 18.6% said that they belonged to SPIDR. It is unclear what the 5.1% who claimed membership in ALRA meant.

9. Valerie A. Personick, "Job Outlook Through 1995: Industry Output and Employment Projections," Monthly Labor Review, Nov. 1981, p. 26, and O. Flaim, "Data on Union Members," Employment and Earnings, Jan. 1985, p. 209.

10. The 1953 figure represents private sector labor force only; in 1984 only 15.6% of the private sector workers were union members while 6.1% of those employed in the public sector were unionized: Myron Lieberman, Public-Sector Bargaining: A Policy Reappraisal (Lenox: Mass.: D.C. Heath & Co., 1980) pp. 2, 4, citing Bureau of Labor Statistics, Directory of National Unions and Employee Associations for 1973, 1975, 1980; Larry T. Adams, "Changing Employment Patterns of Organized Workers," Monthly Labor Review, Feb. 1985, p. 26. The figures given by Leo Troy and Neil Sheflin in U.S. Union Sourcebook: Membership, Finances, Structure, Directory (West Orange, N.J.: Industrial Relations Data and Information Services,

1985), pp. 3-10, 3-14, 3-20, A-1, A-2, are based on union reports under the Landrum-Griffith Act and generally are larger than those reported by the BLS.

11. The Yeshiva decision concerned private institutions under NLRB jurisdiction. Nonetheless, in spring 1987 a hearing examiner for the Pennsylvania Labor Relations Board decided that University of Pittsburgh full-time faculty had managerial authority and hence could not bargain collectively under state law; Chronicle of Higher Education, May 13, 1987, pp. 16ff. Similar challenges occurred in other public institutions.

12. Jewel and Bernard Bellush, Union Power and New York: Victor Gotbaum and District Council 37 (New York: Praeger [1984]), p. 1; Arnold M. Zack, "Impasses, Strikes, and Resolutions," in Sam Zagora, ed. Public Workers and Public Unions (Englewood Cliffs, N.J.: Prentice Hall, 1972), pp. 101-102; Lee C. Shaw, "The Development of State and Federal Laws," Zagora, pp. 20-36.

13. Weinberg, "An Administrative," Weisenfeld, ASMA publications dating from the 1950s and 1960s; Deborah Kolb, The Mediators. By 1985 over forty states had public employment laws, but only 14 of the 33 agencies that responded to the ALRA survey provided staff mediation service in the private sector and 11 in the public sector. Some others provided ad hoc mediators.

14. Herbert Fishgold, "Dispute Resolution in the Public Sector: The Role of the FMCS," Labor Law Review, Dec. 1976, p. 732; Jerome H. Ross, "Federal Mediation in Public Service," Monthly Labor Review, Feb. 1976, pp. 41-45.

15. The first public employment bill was drafted by the American Federation of State, County and Municipal Employees and was introduced in April 1970 by Representative Jacob H. Gilbert (Democrat, New York), while the last was introduced in January 1977 by Representative Edward R. Roybal (Democrat, California). See Government Employment Relations Reporter, (hereafter, GERR) Reference File, 51:181, and GERR, 631 (Nov. 10, 1975): B-6 for proposals to amend the NLRA.

16. 426 US 833; GERR 693 (Jan. 31, 1977): 12; <u>Garcia v. San Antonio Metropolitan Transit Authority</u>, nos. 82-1913 and 82-1915, Supplement to <u>Labor Law Reporter</u>, vol. 118, no. 13 (Feb. 19, 1985); Roger E. Dahl in SPIDR, <u>Neutrals Response to a Society in Dispute: A Multi-track Conference on Dispute Resolution.   1980   Proceedings,   Eighth   Annual Meeting, Oct. 19-22, 1980.   Washington, D. C.</u> (hereafter, SPIDR, 1980), p. 105, on the satisfaction of public employees with the status quo.

17. Reported in GERR, 676 (Sept. 27, 1976): F 1-7; GERR, 703 (April 11, 1977): 30-32. PSRC was closely associated with Americans Against Union Control of Government; GERR, 755: 15-18.

18. GERR, 740:10; 870:10, and 51-52. For the FMCS reply to the GAO, see <u>Labor Law Journal</u>, March 1981, p. 192, and GERR, 894:49-54; <u>Selected Proceedings of the 32nd Annual Conference of the Association of Labor Relations Agencies (July 17-22, 1983, Moncton, New Brunwswick</u> (hereafter, ALRA, 1983), p. 58.

19. Kay McMurray, "The Federal Mediation and Conciliation Service: Serving Labor-Management Relations in the Eighties," <u>Labor Law Journal</u>, Nov. 1981, 745-46; GERR, 955 (March 22, 1982), 12; 937, 11-12.   Reorganization described in ALRA, 32 (1983): 14-17.

20. FMCS figures reported in GERR: 894 and 54. ALRA data from Sept. 1984 is less complete, but it shows virtually the same distribution; preliminary report presented at the annual meeting, July 28, 1985, Portland, Maine.

CHAPTER 3. PORTRAIT OF THE LABOR MEDIATOR

Introduction

"It is a 'lonely' job," remarked one mediator from the midwest as he thanked the Rutgers Institute of Management and Labor Relations "for th[e] opportunity to share feelings" provided by their survey of mediator backgrounds, self-image and attitudes. Another grateful respondent found that the questions encouraged him to "think of what it is I do for a living."

Just who filled this lonely job in 1985 and what they thought about their work is the subject of the present chapter. In it we present a composite portrait of the 1985 mediators, highlighting significant differences between state and federal staff members and between FMCS regions. We show the extent to which their demographic characteristics have changed since the early 1960s, and we look at how they viewed their past career and future prospects.

The 1985 Mediator

The statistically "average" mediator of the 1980s was a middle-aged (45-54 year old) married male with less than one child at home.[1] His career reflected the American tradition of upward social mobility; whereas the most commonly reported parental occupation was skilled worker or foreman (22.7%)[2] and over half of the respondents' fathers failed to complete high school, the mediator had earned a baccalaureate and had taken some graduate courses (Figure 1).[3] He was a "joiner"; he belonged to at least one professional organization and probably was a member either of two or more professional societies or of one work related voluntary association and one or more social, political or religious organization.

Our hypothetical mediator belonged to a union for seven to ten years and was at one time a paid union employee. The second most commonly reported work experience was labor relations position in industry (39%), while 29% of the mediators had held managerial or supervisory posts.

27

FIGURE 1. <u>Highest Educational Achievement</u>

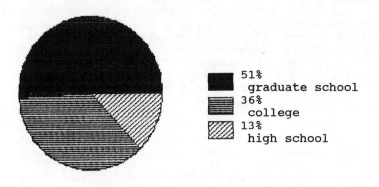

The average mediator was no newcomer. He had worked at his present agency for seven to ten years and had spent up to an additional three years in another agency.   He earned between $45,000 and $49,999, and his family income aver-

FIGURE 2. <u>1984 Salary and Income</u>
(in percentages)

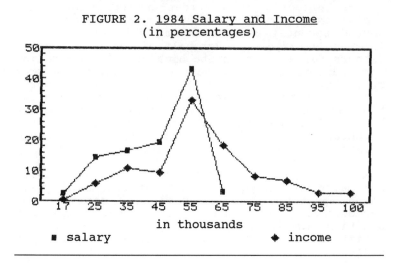

aged an additional $10,000 a year (Figure 2).
More than three-quarters of the respondents had
outside sources of income, and a quarter had more
than one additional source.

This composite portrait masks important differences among mediators. Recruitment patterns
evidently had changed over the years, and state
agency requirements differed. Only one of the administrators said, in response to a separate questionnaire, that his agency expected more than
three years related employment, and most permitted
candidates for entry level positions to substitute
education for part or all of the practical experience. Those agencies which had flexible requirements generally had their own training programs.

The type of employment experience that candidates presented changed over the quarter century
between 1960 and 1985. In 1985 although most newly hired mediators had worked at one time or another in the industrial relations system, in
unions or in industries, an increasing number of
them had worked for government agencies or had had
independent practices as lawyers, labor relations
consultants or neutrals.[4]

Indeed, after 1970 there was a steady decline
in the percentage of mediators who had the direct
industrial relations experience that was gained by
working for unions or for industry. Thus, among
the respondents to the 1985 survey, 41% of the
mediators with less than four years experience had
held a paid union position as compared with 60%
of those with ten to fifteen years of experience.[5]
While 30% of the newly hired mediators had held
labor relations positions in industry and 28% had
served in supervisory or management capacities,
the figures for mediators hired between 1970 and
1975 were 43% and 31% respectively.[6]

As their prior work experience might indicate, the new mediators in 1985 were better educated than those who had been hired in previous
years. Thus 59% of those most recently employed
had earned graduate degrees, while only 32% of the
mediators with four to nine years service in the
same agency had completed their graduate studies.
Among the more seasoned mediators the percentage

of degree holders ranged between twenty (for those
with ten to fifteen years service) and twenty-six
(over fifteen years experience). Not surprisingly, there was a similar relationship between
chronological age and education; younger mediators
were better educated than older ones regardless of
length of service.

Perhaps the differences between mediators who
had served more or less than five years reflected,
at least in part, differences between state and
federal policies because two-thirds of the newly
hired mediators worked for state agencies. Not
only did FMCS and state mediators demonstrate dis-
tinct demographic characteristics, but the length
of service, the type of work that they did and the
type of cases that they handled were also different. As will be discussed later, some differences
also existed between the staff of the several FMCS
regions. But these were not as great as the differences between state and federal employees.

State mediators were younger than their colleagues in the FMCS (Figure 3), were more likely
to be single or divorced and to support three or
more children. Twenty percent of the state
respondents were women, while only 5.5% of the
FMCS participants were female.

As measured by the parents' occupational and
educational achievements, state mediators came
from a slightly higher social level. More of
their parents were owners, managers or professionals (35.5% as opposed to 26%), and their
fathers probably had completed high school (73% as
compared with 66%). Among the federal mediators,
the staff of the Southern Region came from a somewhat higher social level than did their colleagues
(78% of their parents had held skilled or professional jobs as compared with the FMCS average
of 57%). Mediators in the Western Region, for
their part, came from a lower social level than
the others.

State mediators were more gregarious than
their FMCS colleagues, although the clientele evidently exercised more of an influence than agency
affiliation; among both state and FMCS staff,
those mediators who handled public sector cases

FIGURE 3. Age, by Agency, 1985
(by percentage)

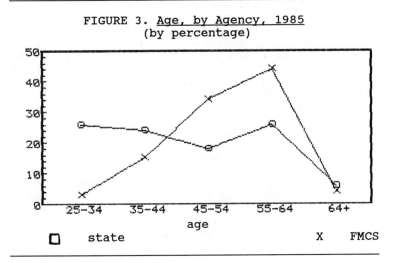

belonged to more voluntary organizations than did
their colleagues who handled private sector
cases.[8]

        More than half of the state mediators had
earned graduate degrees. Contrary to what might
have been expected, the educational background of
federal mediators did not increase over the years,
although all of the respondents hired since 1979
had some college training. The group with the
highest educational qualifications consisted of
those mediators who had served 25 or more years at
the time of the survey, two-thirds of whom had
attended graduate school. The least well educated
were those hired between 1967 and 1969 (sixteen to
eighteen years service). Of these, 30% had not
attended college, including one who had received
only a grade school education.[9]

        Within the FMCS, Eastern and Central district
mediators attained higher educational levels than
their Southern and Western colleagues. Forty percent of the respondents from the Central Region
had attended graduate school, and 28.6% of the
mediators from both the Central and Eastern regions had some college education. On the other
hand, two-thirds of the respondents who reported

that they had never attended college were employed
by the Southern and Central regions.

Unlike their federal colleagues, less than
half of the state mediators had been employed by a
union (40% state and 62% FMCS respondents). They
were far more likely to have had experience as
teachers, lawyers, neutrals or independent labor
relations consultants for unions (but not for industry). The chances were also greater that they
had worked for a government agency sometime in the
past (23% as compared with 8%).

Among Federal mediators, those from the
Central Region had the most diverse work experience. Although 42% had worked for manufacturing
or retail establishments, their prior employment
experience included all of the categories (professional practice, education, government, public
service, military and political). This was true
of no other region.

State staff members had less mediation experience than their federal colleagues. On the average they had worked four to six years at their
current agency and between seven and nine years as
mediators. Whereas almost one-third (32%) of all
federal mediators had been with the service for
more than fifteen years, less than 15% of the
state mediators enjoyed such tenure.

State mediators appeared more likely than
their federal counterparts to move from one
mediation agency to another. Thus, almost the
same percent of FMCS employees reported having
sixteen or more years experience both with their
current agency and with any agency (32.1% and
32.8% respectively). The comparable figures for
state mediators were both lower and more widely
separated (14.6% and 19.8%).

FMCS figures on length of service masked a
significant difference between regional offices.
During the 1960s, when collective bargaining began
to spread throughout the South, the FMCS office
evidently recruited experienced mediators from
within the service; 26.5% of the respondents from
that area reported nineteen or more years mediation experience, while only 20.6% had served that
long in the same agency. From the figures, it

appears likely that the mediators came from what
is now the Central Region.

Mediator salaries varied widely (Figure 2,
above). For state mediators, the beginning salary
ranged from $12,000 to $38,000 and maximums went
from $23,000 to $55,000.[10] Their average fell
between $30,000 and $34,999.

Federal salaries were considerably higher
than those paid by state agencies (Figure 4); the
average FMCS mediator earned $20,000 more than his
state colleague. Other income narrowed the gap;
the typical federal mediator earned an additional
$5,000 annually from outside sources, while a
combination of investments and secondary employment by self and spouse provided the average state
mediator with a welcome $15,000 a year.

There were significant differences in family
income between FMCS regions. Forty-one percent of
the Eastern respondents reported incomes above
$70,000 as compared with 15.3% of the Western
mediators. This reflects the fact that, on the
average, mediators from the Eastern Region had
worked the longest for the agency, while those
from the Western Region had the shortest period of
service.

Current duties and type of cases distinguished the state and federal mediator even more
than demographic characteristics and work experience. While 90% of all FMCS staff devoted all or
almost full-time to mediation, barely one-half of
the state respondents were able to do so. The re-
mainder reported that they spend at least half of
their time on administrative or labor board
activities.

By 1985 a rough division of labor had developed between FMCS and state agencies whereby
state mediators concentrated on public sector
disputes and the FMCS handled most private sector
cases. Although the proportion varied according
to local legislation, 82% of the participating
state mediators characterized their case load as
consisting all or mostly of public sector disputes. Less than 10% of the federal mediators
reported a preponderance of public sector cases
even though they mediated disputes involving

FIGURE 4. <u>1984 Salary and Income, by Agency</u>
(by percentages)

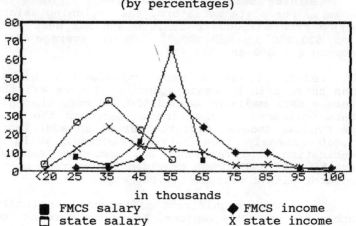

in thousands

■ FMCS salary   ◆ FMCS income
□ state salary   X state income

public employees in states that lacked their own
agencies (Table 1). Within the FMCS, respondents
from the Eastern Region reported the greatest
concentration on private sector cases (97%), while
those from the Central Region reported the lowest
(85%).[11]

TABLE 1. <u>Type of Cases Normally Handled,</u>
<u>by Agency</u>
(in percentages)

Type	FMCS	State	Total
all public sector	0	27.1	11.5
mostly public sector	5.5	55.2	24.9
mostly private sector	71.2	8.3	45.1
all private sector	16.4	4.2	11.5
no response	6.8	5.2	7.1

Federal mediators had mixed feelings about
their involvement in the public sector. While one
mediator thought that the service "should be out

of the pub. sect.," another wrote: "I like public
sector cases because they are often visible cases
and contribute to enhancing the image of the parties." It will be interesting to investigate in
the next chapter what effect the difference in
types of cases that the mediators ordinarily
handled had upon their attitudes toward the mediation process and various professional issues.

Changes over a Quarter Century

At first glance the 1985 professional mediator looked very much like his 1960s counterpart.
At both dates the profession was dominated by
middle-aged married men who had belonged to and
worked for a union at some time during their
career.

Even the salary levels were similar. When
adjusted for changes in the consumer price index,
the 1964 FMCS mediator earned $47,803 and the me-
dian income for a 1962 state mediator was $33,900.
The comparable figures for 1985 fell between
$45,000 and $49,999 for FMCS and between $30,000
and $34,999 for state employees. Figures 4
(above) and 5 show, however, that the distribution
changed dramatically, as did the importance of additional income.[12]

There were other changes as well, as mediation became a less exclusively masculine occupation. Whereas in 1962 only one woman responded to
the state survey, twenty years later 19% or 20% of
the participating state mediators were women. The
1964 FMCS questionnaire did not even ask gender;
in 1985 there were eight (5.5%) female respondents, although the Southern Region had none.

Additional differences become apparent as the
data is studied more closely. In the 1960s the
age distribution of state and federal mediators
described a curve which peaked between 45 and 54
years. In 1985, while the general shape of the
federal curve was similar, it peaked between 55
and 64. The age distribution of state mediators
changed even more dramatically. Instead of
forming a bell-shaped curve, it had two peaks, one
representing the quarter of the respondents who
fell between the ages of 25 and 45 and the other

the quarter who were between 55 and 64 years
(Figure 6).

FIGURE 5. <u>1960s Salary and Income, by Agency</u>
(by percentages)

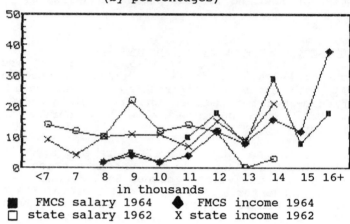

        <7   7   8   9   10   11   12   13   14   15 16+
                        in thousands
    ■ FMCS salary 1964   ◆ FMCS income 1964
    ☐ state salary 1962   X state income 1962

The 1985 federal mediator not only was older
than his predecessor, he also had served longer in
the FMCS.   In the early 1960s the federal service
evidently had undergone a recent hiring spurt; 23%
of its mediators had been employed only one to
three years.   At the other end of the scale, another 27% had been with the agency for nineteen or
more years.   In 1985, less than one-tenth of the
federal mediators had been hired during the previous three years, a little less than one-half had
joined the service between 1973 and 1978, and a
third dated back to the mid-sixties.

On the whole, length of service among state
mediators changed less than FMCS tenure.   Perhaps
the average state staff member in 1985 had served
a year or two longer than his 1962 counterpart,
but the difference was too small to be significant.   Interestingly enough, a quarter of a century before, state mediators tended to have had
slightly more overall mediation experience than

they did in 1985, but the difference was not ।
great.

FIGURE 6. <u>Mediators' Ages, by Agency</u>
<u>1960s and 1985</u>
(by percentages)

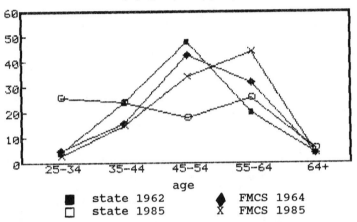

state 1962 ■   FMCS 1964 ◆
state 1985 □   FMCS 1985 X

Conclusions: Qualifications and Professionalism

Having taken this rather detailed look at the
1985 mediator and having compared him to his 1960s
counterpart, can we conclude that the efforts to
increase professionalism among mediators was successful? Were the newer mediators indeed better
prepared than their predecessors had been?

The answer to these questions is a tentative
yes, at least in so far as professionalization is
defined by post-secondary education. The response
is less obvious if professionalism is defined by
career-related work experience.

Thus, although the 1985 mediators were better
educated, fewer of them came to mediation from
industrial or union labor relations positions, and
they might perhaps have been regarded as less well
qualified than their 1960s counterparts. If, however, the shift in the type of cases that state
mediators handled from private to public sector is

taken into account, then one might argue that
experience in a labor-related government agency
provided excellent preparation for mediating disputes between public employees and their government employers. It was appropriate that 25% of
all mediators involved in the public sector had
worked for one or another government labor board,
while only 7% of the mediators who handled all or
mostly all private sector disputes had had such
experience.

More public sector mediators had previously
held industrial labor relations, managerial or
supervisory positions than had the mediators whose
work fell primarily in the private sector. It is
significant, moreover, that private sector mediators were far more likely (62%) to have been employed by a union than were their public sector
colleagues (39)%.

Thus, there was an increasing differentiation
in qualifications between those whose cases fell
primarily in the public or in the private sector.
Traditional union/management relations shed less
light on the sometimes complex issues involved in
government employment situations, and it was appropriate that mediators who handled public sector
cases had more experience with government labor
relations agencies and with the practice of law.

Over the years mediators had seen the need
for improved training of new recruits, and the
FMCS developed an elaborate program. Unfortunately, agency retrenchment, which prevented the
federal service from hiring new staff for several
years, made this less important.

State agencies, which continued to hire, had
fewer facilities.[13] This was a problem that ALRA
and SPIDR alike attempted to alleviate, and it is
interesting to note that membership in these two
associations was considerably higher among state
than among FMCS staff, while a larger proportion
of the federal mediators belonged to the research-
oriented IRRA.

What is obvious, therefore, is a growing differentiation in educational background and prior
experience between mediators employed by the FMCS
and by state agencies, with somewhat less of a

difference between FMCS regions. Considering the increased difference in the type of cases that they handled, it would be wrong to say that one group was more professional or better prepared than another.

The description given in this chapter of the extent to which the 1985 FMCS and state mediators differed in background and demographic character- istics from each other and from the mediators a quarter century before shows the evolution of a dynamic profession. It also provides the basis for investigating whether changing external and internal conditions affected mediators' attitudes toward their job (in Chapters 4 and 7) and in Chapters 5, 6 and 8, toward unions, the American industrial relations system and the mediation process itself. In addition, the comparison of FMCS responses by region provides some clues as to whether geographic differences exercised a signi- ficant influence on respondents' attitudes towards their job and their career.

1. For age, see Figure 3 below. Eighty-three percent of the respondents were married, 5.8% single, 1.7% widowed, and 9.2% divorced and separated. FMCS marriages appeared to be more stable; only 5.5% reported divorce or separations as compared with 14.7% of the state mediators.

2. Two or more parental occupations were reported by 8.2% of the respondents. The questionnaire was justly criticized for failing to ask the mother's educational level. The largest categories were semi-skilled (18%) and skilled labor (23%), owner (16%) and professional (14%).

3. The educational level of all mediators was far higher than that of the American civilian labor force; 77% of the state and 53% of the FMCS mediators as compared with 23% of the entire labor force had completed college. For educational accomplishments of the American labor force see Anne McDougall Young, "One-fourth of the Adult Labor Force are College Graduates," Monthly Labor Review, Feb. 1985, pp. 43-46.

4. Of the mediators hired since 1981, 22% reported experience in government service as compared with 14% of those hired during the 1970s. The figures for independent practice were as follows: for mediators with less than four years experience: lawyer, 28%, neutral, 15%, and industrial consultant, 15%. For mediators with 10 to 15 years experience: law practice, 1%, neutral, 14%, industrial consultant, 9%. The comparison with mediators who had more than 15 years experience was even more extreme.

5. Among the respondents to the 1985 Rutgers survey, union experience was inversely related to education. Ninety-one percent of the respondents with a high school education had belonged to a union, whereas the figures for college and graduate school attenders was 71% and 31% respectively.

6. It should be remembered that the FMCS hired almost no mediators between 1980 and 1985 and that mediators who in 1985 had less than four years

experience served in state agencies. According to former FMCS Commissioner Edward P. Hartfield, as late as 1982, that service still preferred to hire mediators who had had actual experience at the bargaining table, although it had employed some whose only experience had been with other neutral agencies: "Becoming a Mediator," Creative Approaches to Dispute Resolution. 1982 Proceedings, Tenth Annual Conference, Society of Professionals in Dispute Resolution, Oct. 17-19, 1982. Detroit, Mich., p. 94 (hereafter SPIDR, 1982). In its Sept. 1985 vacancy announcement, the FMCS required a minimum of seven years of "full-time progressively responsible and successful experience in collective bargaining negotiations or the equivalent in other closely allied fields of labor-management relations" although the Service did consider substituting educational and/or non-labor dispute resolution experience for three of the seven years; information supplied by Paul Yager.

The revised edition of Simkin's classic work, Mediation and the Dynamics of Collective Bargaining, discusses the latest FMCS requirements. See also: Thomas A. Kochin, Collective Bargaining and Industrial Relations: From Theory to Policy and Practice (Homewood, Ill.: Richard D. Irwin, Inc., [1980]), p. 286, and Harold Newman in Public Employment Relations Services, Portrait of a Process: Collective Negotiations in Public Employment (Fort Washington, Pa.: Labor Relations Press, [1979]), p. 198; Zack, pp. iv, 14.

7. All of the female FMCS respondents to this survey were hired after 1972. Although the Southern Region hired 20 staff mediators between 1973 and 1985, none of them was female.

8. Seventy-four percent of the state mediator respondents reported membership in at least one organization, as did 66% percent of the participating FMCS staff. The diffence increased when responses were classified by types of cases handled: 78% of the mediators who usually handled public sector cases reported membership, as did 62% of those who handled private sector disputes. The distinction between public and private sector will be discussed more fully below. Since, however, 86% of the public sector mediators worked for state agencies, the categories "state" and "public sector" tended to exhibit the same

demographic characteristics; association membership was one of the few areas where a greater difference by type of cases indicates that the factor
"clientele" might have exerted a greater influence
than "agency affiliation."

9. Generalizations are hazardous in that only 14
of the 142 mediators who answered this question
were hired after 1979. One might ask whether the
fact that all of the respondents with 22 or more
years of agency experience had attended college
reflects hiring policy or a higher retirement/
resignation rate among those with fewer educational qualifications.

10. Replies by 16 agency administrators to a separate questionnaire.

11. Since FMCS mediators were organized into large
geographic regions, it was impossible to identify
responses of those who worked in such states as
Florida, Ohio and Illinois as had enacted public
sector collective bargaining laws but had failed
to appoint state mediators.

12. The CPI increased 347.7% between 1985 and
1962, when the data for state mediators was collected, and 356.6% since 1964, the date of the
original federal survey. Unless stated otherwise,
comparisons are based on the figures given in the
two earlier studies by Indik and Berkowitz. Unfortunately, it was impossible to present this
comparison in tabular form, but Figures 4 and 5
show the distribution in the 1960s and in 1985.
Salaries in 1985 fell within a narrower range.
Although the graphs indicate that additional income had increased the gap, this might have been
due to the failure in the 1960s to provide sufficient categories at the upper end of the scale.

13. Survey conducted by ALRA in 1985; Zack, pp.
14, 15, 183.

Having seen the extent to which mediators changed between the 1960s and 1985, we will now look at how these changes influenced their view of themselves, their past careers and their future prospects. To what extent did the disillusioned or critical comments appended to several of the questionnaires reflect the feelings of state and federal mediators? Several approaches have been used to answer these questions.[1]

Job Satisfaction

Two questions broached the subject directly. Participants were asked: "Considering your job as a whole, how well do you like it?" and "Looking back over your career as realistically as possible, how well would you say you have done?" None of the respondents admitted to disliking his or her job although 15% expressed mixed feelings about it. More than two-thirds were very satisfied. On the whole, FMCS mediators reported greater satisfaction than did state mediators (76% were very satisfied as compared with 58%). Among FMCS, the Easterners expressed the most satisfaction (94% as compared with 76% for the least pleased group, the Westerners).

Nonetheless, the uncertainties expressed in individual mediator comments evidently had taken their toll; job satisfaction declined, especially among state mediators. The proportion of those who reported that they were very satisfied fell by 18% between 1962 and 1985. It should be noted, moreover, that spontaneous comments on federal questionnaires indicated that a minority of FMCS mediators, in particular from the Southern region, were strongly aggrieved by conditions within that agency (issues pertaining specifically to FMCS matters will be discussed below).

In general, there appears to be a cycle in job satisfaction. Euphoria reigned for the first year when 81.5% of the respondents reported high satisfaction, followed by a period of disillusionment when the percent of very satisfied respondents among those who had served between one and

43

three years dropped to 53.   After 12 years the
percent once again rose above 70 (Figure 1).

    Slightly more than half of all mediators be-
lieved that they had done better or much better in
their careers than they had expected.   The figures
for state and federal mediators were almost the
same; 50% for state and 52% for FMCS staff members.   Among the FMCS, the Southerners expressed
the most satisfaction with their careers and the
Westerners expressed the least.

    Surprisingly enough, in view of the decline
in overall job satisfaction, the 1985 mediators
viewed their careers more favorably than did their
counterparts in the 1960s.   At the earlier date,
38% of the federal and 43% of the state mediators
rated their careers as better than anticipated,
whereas a quarter century later, the figures were

FIGURE 1. <u>Job Satisfaction, by Years at Agency,</u>
<u>1985</u>*
(in percentages)

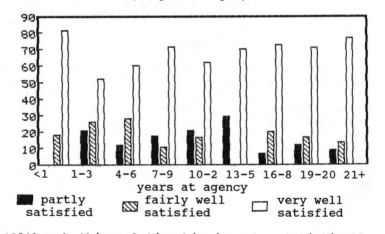

partly satisfied   fairly well satisfied   very well satisfied

*Although this relationship is not statistically
significant (significance level less than .25),
the   figures   indicate an   interesting   trend.
The question of significance is discussed   below
in Appendix A: "A Note on Statistical Methods."

152% and 50% respectively. This change can, perhaps, be attributed to a decline in alternative
employment opportunities.

When asked to what they attributed their success or lack thereof, more than half of the mediators replied that the organizations had treated
them fairly as distinguished from generously or
poorly.[2]   There was no real difference between
state and federal sentiments on this question. A
majority of both groups also believed that they
had done alright or well on their own.

It is not surprising that in 1985 almost
twice as many state as federal mediators believed
that their education was an advantage, while the
proportions were reversed between mediators who
regarded their education as unimportant. Twenty-
five years earlier, when the average mediator was
less well educated, he attributed very little of
his success to education. In fact, since he rated
his career lower than did the 1985 mediator, he
was less likely to cite a positive reason for his
success.

Job satisfaction can be measured indirectly
by looking at the mediators' career expectations.
Did they want to stay at the same agency, or
indeed in the field of mediation? Measured this
way, there was a striking difference between
federal and state mediators; 69% of the FMCS
intended to remain mediators,[3] while only 45% of
the state staff members expressed a similar
intention (Figure 2).[4] In the 1960s mediation had
been somewhat more attractive to federal mediators
and considerably more so to the employees of state
agencies.

Looking at the data in another way, mediators
who in 1985 reported high job satisfaction wanted
and expected to stay in mediation, but in a higher
position with increased pay. Up to a certain
point, satisfied mediators expected to earn higher
salaries in 1990 than did their less happy colleagues, but a few of those expressing low satisfaction expected by 1990 to earn more than $70,000
(the then upper limit of FMCS salaries, and well
above what state mediators were earning in 1985).[5]

FIGURE 2. <u>Future Career Plans: 1960s and 1985</u>
(in percentages)

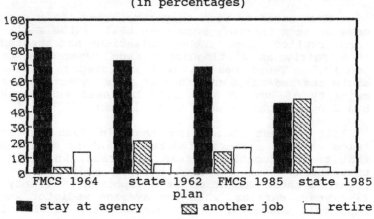

The desire to stay in mediation was also related to age and education. Mediators who were
younger than 35 and had a college education were
less interested in remaining, while middle-aged
ones were more enthusiastic about the prospect
(see Chapter 8).

Job satisfaction has long been the subject of
popular speculation as well as intensive study by
industrial psychologists. Some of the factors
which are believed to contribute to a happy labor
force are: adequate salaries, the belief that
skills are being employed properly, good relations
with clients (co-workers, supervisors), task
variety, job security and satisfactory career
prospects.

More 1985 mediators either were satisfied or
dissatisfied with their salary than was the case
in the 1960s (more than twice as many respondents
in 1985 than in the 1960s selected the extreme
responses of "very dissatisfied/completely satisfied": 24.5% as compared with 56.5%). Considering
the difference in pay, it is not surprising that
federal mediators were happier with their income
than their state colleagues (70% as compared with
50% were moderately or completely satisfied). But

they insisted that wages had more than personal
significance. One mediator explained:

> An important aspect leading to the suc-
> cessful performance of the mediator is
> his/her own self-assessment. I would have
> to say that the disparity in the pay of
> the mediator vs. the clients he deals with
> day-in and day-out have to have a signifi-
> cant affect on the mediator's impor-
> tance.[6]

Among the 1985 mediators, job satisfaction
was, on the whole, related to attitudes toward
wages. Thus 71% of the "very satisfied" mediators
were completely or moderately content with their
salaries, while only 37% of those reporting mixed
feelings about their job were satisfied with what
they earned (Table 1).

TABLE 1. Job Satisfaction,
by Salary Satisfaction: 1985*

Degree of salary satisfaction

Job satisfaction	completely/ moderately satisfied	slightly satisfied/ so-so/ slightly dissatisfied	completely/ moderately dissatis- fied
so-so	36.9	29.0	34.3
fairly satisfied	50.2	27.5	22.5
very satisfied	70.7	20.1	9.2

*This relationship is statistically significant
(at the <.004 level).

There was one exception, however. Although
new hires reported the highest level of job satisfaction, they also expressed the greatest amount
of dissatisfaction with their income. Evidently
low wages did not immediately affect their attitudes, but as early enthusiasm wore off, their

overall reaction reflected their unhappiness with
their pay.

Federal and state mediators reported approximately the same degree of satisfaction with the
use to which their skills were put and with the
variety that they experienced on the job, even
though state staff members engaged in less mediation and were assigned other labor board functions. Compared with the 1960s, state as well as
federal mediators reported less variety (55% of
both groups reported "a great deal" of variety in
1985, whereas in the 1960s 73% of the FMCS and 66%
of the state mediators selected that response).
Their perception is interesting because both
groups preferred a job that was constantly changing, and the very satisfied mediators reported
more variety than did their less satisfied colleagues.[7]

Variety is one of the characteristics included in a "risk preference" scale designed to
measure how willing various occupational groups
are to accept work-related insecurity. State and
federal mediators ranked high on this scale,
demonstrating a strong preference for occupations
that involved greater than average risks. Interestingly, however, mediators chose low scoring alternatives to questions concerning willingness to
confront challenges and to accept a job that might
not last (45% and 61% respectively). As in the
1960s, state mediators were more risk oriented,
although the gap between the two groups had narrowed considerably, and, in comparison with other
occupations studied in the mid-1960s, mediators
were most likely to prefer a responsible, exciting, but insecure position (Figure 3).[8]

There was a significant difference between
state and federal mediators in another job dimension, their reaction to the clients with whom
they worked. While 80% of the FMCS participants
said that they very much liked "meeting and
mediating" with the labor and management people
with whom they "worked from time to time," only
53% of the state mediators were equally pleased.[9]
These figures show a marked decline from the 1960s
when 90% of the federal and 85% of the state
mediators said that they liked working with their
clients very much.

This change is important because, of all the variables selected for analysis, attitude toward working with clients showed the strongest relationship with job satisfaction. Thus 94% of the mediators who were very satisfied with their job liked their regular client relationships very much; the other 5% liked them fairly well. Moreover, the degree to which they were satisfied with their client relationships explained the difference between federal and state mediators' expressed job satisfaction and most of the difference between public and private sector mediators on this point (Chapter 8). Presumably state mediators found working with government officials less interesting or rewarding than private sector mediators found working with corporate managers.

FIGURE 3. <u>Willingness to Accept Job Related Risks</u>,
           <u>by Agency, 1960s and 1985</u>*
              (percent of responses)

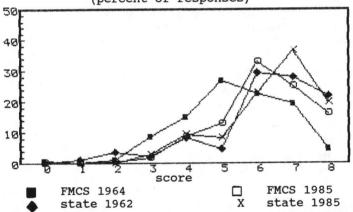

| ■ | FMCS 1964 | □ | FMCS 1985 |
| ◆ | state 1962 | X | state 1985 |

*Each respondent was assigned a score based on responses to a series of questions measuring preference for risky situations. A low score indicates a preference for secure situations, while a high score shows a willingness to risk failure or insecurity.

There also was a noticeable, although less strong, relationship between job satisfaction and optimism concerning the possibility of fulfilling career goals. Of the mediators who said they were very satisfied with their job, 70% thought that there was an excellent or good chance of achieving their goals as compared with the 56% who had mixed feelings about their job. Comparable figures were not available for the 1960s.

A final dimension often emphasized by students of mediation is job stress.[10] Participants in the survey were asked whether they were frequently, sometimes or rarely, or never bothered by a series of work related conditions (see Appendix B, questions 55-69). All thirteen items disturbed one respondent or another, and state mediators were bothered by more items than were their FMCS colleagues. While the most frequently checked alternative was lack of informational materials (12% of the federal mediators were frequently bothered by this), both state and federal mediators showed increasing concern over lack of authority and unclear responsibility (Table 2). Still, they were less bothered in 1985 than they had been twenty-five years ago about career related issues and conflicting loyalties.

TABLE 2. Job Stress:
Authority and Responsibility
(in percentages)

	1962/64			1985		
	rarely/ never	some- times	fre- quently	rarely/ never	some- times	fre- quently
bothered by:						
lack authority						
FMCS	83	15	2	70	27	3
State	72	23	5	63	29	8
unclear responsibility						
FMCS	89	10	1	77	20	3
State	82	13	5	76	22	2

In general, although the 1985 median score on the stress scale was the same as it had been in

the earlier study (Table 3) and although state
mediators continued to find their work more
stressful, the combined percentage point difference between the two groups decreased from 44% to
36%, indicating that their reaction had become
somewhat more similar.

TABLE 3. Job Stress, by Agency: 1960s and 1985
(in percentages)

	1962/64		1985	
Score*	FMCS	State	FMCS	State
13-16	34	13	32	24
17-20	31	30	26	29
21-24	20	27	33	22
25-28	8	16	10	19
29-32	4	10	4	6
above 32	3	4	5	8

*Each respondent was given a score based on res-
ponses to a series of questions which measure job
stress. "Rarely" or "never" responses were rated
as 1, "sometimes" received 3 points, and "frequently bothered" responses rated 5 points. Omitted items were assigned the score of 1 as the most
frequently selected alternative. A low score indicates a high tolerance for stress and vice-
versa.

Significant differences existed between the
FMCS regions in terms of reaction to job stress.
Southern mediators evidently found their work less
stressful than their colleagues from other
regions; their score was the lowest on one-half of
the 14 questions that measured this factor and
tied for lowest on another, while their overall
score was also the lowest. Respondents from the
Central Region scored the highest on eight questions, but Western respondents had the highest
total score.[11]

Interestingly enough, despite their concern
about job stress, more than half of the mediators
from the Western Region claimed to prefer a job

which offered high excitement and low security.
On the other hand, 81% of the mediators from the
Central Region, who also appeared concerned about
job stress, preferred a position which had little
excitement but high security.

In addition to the questions asked of the
state and, in Canada, the provincial mediators,
the survey contained three questions concerning
matters of interest to FMCS staff only.   They
were: "National Office staff or representatives
can at times be helpful in resolving difficult
disputes by active participation"; "When a National Office Representative is working with a field
mediator on a case, the former should always act
as chairman of the Panel"; and "Regional Directors
and Assistants should never participate in joint
bargaining sessions."

While respondents from the Eastern Region
found National Office assistance to be the most
valuable (85% did so as compared with an average
of 75% of all FMCS respondents), they were less,
but not the least, willing to let a representative
of the National Office chair the panel (59% were
unwilling as compared with the average of
54.5%).[12]   On both of the questions measuring
attitudes toward the National Office, mediators
from the Central Region expressed the least appreciation for their assistance (67% found their help
useful, and only 22.5% were willing to let them
chair a mediation panel).[13]

Mediators from the Central Region, moreover,
were less likely to grant their director an active
role in mediation than were the respondents from
the Eastern Region; 35% of the former and 11% of
the latter agreed with the statement that their
directors should not join negotiation sessions
(the average for all regions was 27%).   In addition, the Eastern respondents expressed a low
level of uncertainty on this issue (3% as compared
with the overall average of 12%).

Responses of the Southern mediators to the
questions concerning FMCS issues were close to the
average, but the Southern respondents made the
most comments (35% of the total) as well as the
largest percent (15%) of all remarks on government
policy, most of which were critical.   On the other

hand, Eastern mediators were least likely (.03%)
to comment on government policy even though they
offered the highest percentage (12%) of all statements about professional issues.

Despite the questions that some FMCS mediators raised about the role of their directors and
of the National Office staff members and the
critical remarks made about federal government
policy, most of them apparently believed that they
had been treated fairly by the agency.   The only
group where a comparatively high percentage
(11.5%) believed that they had been treated poorly
was the Western Region (the average was 4%).

The results of the 1964 survey of Federal
mediators were not analyzed by region, and, in any
case, the districts were radically reorganized in
1982.   It therefore is impossible to tell whether
the FMCS staff in the several regions became more
or less satisfied with their relationships with
their directors and with the National Office
staff.

Taking the profession of labor mediation as a
whole, however, the various measures of job satisfaction show that in comparison with the mediators
polled in the 1960s, mediators in 1985 were somewhat less content with their lot.   Lower job satisfaction was linked with their perception that
they had less of an opportunity to use their
skills and that their client-mediator relationships were less satisfactory.   Although there was
no evidence of strong disaffection, in view of the
overall decline in job satisfaction, it will be
interesting to see in Chapter 8 what further analysis can reveal about the 1985 mediators' response
to their work.   First, however, we will look at
their attitude toward several professional issues
in mediation.

1. See Appendix A for discussion of methods. In order to compare results with the 1960s studies, this section discusses first-level relationships only. A more detailed analysis will be made in Chapter 8 below.

2. Responses to this question are difficult to compare with earlier results because the wording used in 1985 evidently conveyed different meanings. More 1960s mediators believed that their organization had done poorly by them, and fewer thought that they had done well on their own.

3. This is not always an accurate measurement of job satisfaction; Eastern FMCS staff expressed the highest level (94%) of satisfaction with their job, but they also gave the lowest (40%) intention of staying in mediation. This seeming contradiction probably is explained by the significant percent (30% as compared with 17% overall) of respondents from the East who intended to retire within the next five years.

4. In order to compare with the 1960s results, slightly different categories were used. The 2.1% of the state and 1.4% of the FMCS respondents who wanted to remain in mediation but to move to another agency were counted as "other." For a more detailed analysis, see Chapter 8.

5. Six. The relationship is not statistically significant.

6. In the 1960s a mediator expressed similar sentiments in almost the same words; see Indik, p. 21.

7. Jerome T. Barrett lists challenge and variety among the major characteristics of the mediator's job; "The Psychology of a Mediator," Occasional Paper No. 83-1, March 1983, SPIDR Committee on Research and Education (Washington, D.C.: SPIDR, [1983]).

8. In 1985 the average score for state mediators was 6.41 (of a possible 8) and for FMCS, 6.14. In the 1960s the comparable figures were: state, 6.2

and FMCS 5.4. At that time public utility managers scored 4.3, graduate students at an Eastern
university, 5.9: Indik, pp. 49-51.

9. The responses to this question rather than to
the question concerning people with whom they
worked regularly are cited in order to compare
results with those published by Indik, p. 49. In
1985 state and federal mediators reported an
increase in satisfaction with their relationship
with regular clients (63.5% as compared with 53.5%
for state mediators in 1962).

10. Hartfield asserts that job stress "is a regular part of our working environment": SPIDR,
1982, p. 96. Kolb's conclusion that the conditions under which state mediators functioned were
more stressful (pp. 15-16) appears to be confirmed
by the mediators' perception of their own jobs.
Barrett discusses in great detail some of the
factors that contribute to job stress.

11. The scores for the two regions ranged from
21.25 to 24.86. The two respondents from the
National Office reported even greater stress;
their score was 25.00.

12. Sixty-five percent of the respondents from the
Western Region opposed.

13. Thirty-one percent of all FMCS respondents
thought that representatives of the National Office should chair the panel. Central Region
mediators expressed a high degree (22%) of uncertainty on this question.

CHAPTER 5.
COLLECTIVE BARGAINING ISSUES

Introduction
       Among both the general public and labor rela-
tions professionals, attitudes toward the industrial relations system that developed under the
NLRA underwent significant changes between the
1960s and 1985. As early as 1976 one knowledge-
able official noted that "the economic and political climate toward collective bargaining has
reached a low ebb." Unions felt threatened by
more aggressive management activity and accused
the NLRB of collusion with employers. On the
other hand, such large corporations as General
Motors and American Telegraph and Telephone worked
with employee organizations to find new ways of
structuring their labor force. While scholarly
observers were unclear whether these were isolated
examples or harbingers of a new industrial relations system, the AFL-CIO executive council committed itself to [1]exploring alternative labor-
management systems.

       In this chapter we will investigate whether
changing economic and political conditions affected mediators' attitudes toward their occupation and the industrial relations system of which
it is a part. We will assess the extent to which
their attitudes were influenced by their previous
employment, the agency for which they worked and
the type of cases that they normally handled.

       The 1966 Rutgers study found significant at-
titudinal differences between mediators employed
by the FMCS on the one hand and the various state
agencies on the other. Subsequently, public sector collective bargaining became increasingly
widespread, particularly at the state level.   It
was argued that by 1980 the real difference among
mediators was caused by the concentration of some
on public sector cases and of others on private
sector disputes.[2]   Using the data from the 1985
survey we will see whether, as the theory pre-
dicts, the differences between mediators who
handled public and private sector disputes were
greater than the earlier distinctions between
state and federal mediators. In addition, we will

look at differences between FMCS regions to see
what impact, if any, geographic influences
exerted.

In Chapter 3 we noted that most public sector
mediation was handled by state mediators, while
FMCS staff usually worked in the private sector
(Chapter 3, Table 1). Consequently, whether the
responses to questions concerning mediation and
the American industrial relations system were
tallied by agency or by the type of cases that the
respondent normally handled made a meaningful difference for only a few questions; further analysis
was necessary in order to determine whether mediators were influenced more by the nature of the
agency for which they worked or by the type of
cases that they normally handled.

Agency affiliation and type of cases were not
the only factors affecting mediator responses to
questions about collective bargaining issues;
union membership exerted a long-lasting influence
as well. Because such experience was common among
both state and FMCS personnel,[3] the extent to
which former membership in or employment by a labor organization changed attitudes can easily be
measured. On other questions distinctive opinions
were held by mediators who had never held labor
relations positions and had less immediate experience with the American industrial relations
system.

In addition to assessing the influence of
agency affiliation and differing backgrounds on
the 1985 mediators' attitudes toward collective
bargaining issues, we will compare their responses
to those reported in the 1960s. We will examine
whether the demographic changes noted in the last
chapter have increased the difference between federal and state mediators and have significantly
altered their attitudes toward their work and the
environment in which they function.

Attitudes toward Unions and the American Collective Bargaining System

The 1962/64 questionnaires asked whether the
respondents believed unions to be obsolete, whether they considered unions to be necessary for
protecting workers and whether they attributed the

high American standard of living to union activities. They also were asked if they believed that
unions made it more difficult for a superior employee to get ahead and if they held unions responsible for inflationary trends. New items were
added in 1985 to measure mediator opinions on such
contemporary issues as whether unions hindered
management attempts to meet the productivity standards set by foreign competitors and whether
unions should help companies faced with economic
hardship.

A comparison of the 1962/64 and 1985 responses revealed an interesting phenomenon. In
the 1960s state mediators expressed more favorable attitudes toward unions than did their federal colleagues. By 1985, however, the attitudes
of the two groups had become more similar and (in
the case of the federal mediator, even) more favorable. The convergence between the two groups
of mediators may perhaps be attributed to the
changing proportion of mediators who at one time
belonged to a union; in the 1960s more state than
federal mediators had been members, whereas in
1985 not only had membership declined among state
mediators, but former membership among FMCS staff
outstripped theirs by 12%. On some questions,
however, difference in union background does not
appear to be statistically significant (see Appendix A for discussion of statistical significance).

FMCS mediators in 1985 took a slightly more
supportive stand on questions that measured attitudes toward unions than did their state colleagues. Thus, for example, almost 100% of the
federal mediators and 90% of their state colleagues denied that unions were obsolete. In the
1960s the percentages were 92% and 97% respectively. In 1985 87.5% of the state and 90% of the
federal mediators believed that the high American
standard of living was largely due to union activities, while a quarter of a century before, 87% of
the state mediators and only 79% of the FMCS staff
agreed with the statement.

For the most part, differences between state
and federal mediators were not large, and the
only item that revealed a marked divergence between the two groups posed the question of whether
unions prevented superior employees from getting

ahead. Only one-fifth of the FMCS respondents agreed with the proposition, while nearly one-third of their state colleagues accepted it. Interestingly enough, in 1962/64 almost 40% of both groups agreed. Employment history helps explain this difference; former paid union workers disagreed most strongly (76%), regardless of agency affiliation, while mediators who had never worked for a union expressed less (60%) disagreement. The difference between the attitudes of mediators who normally handled private and public sector cases followed the same pattern but was not as large.[4]

Within the FMCS, mediators who served in the Western regional office took the most consistently "pro-union" position. The responses of the mediators from the other regions did not follow a consistent pattern; peculiar economic conditions within their areas apparently were stronger than union experiences (Table 1).[5]

TABLE 1. Attitudes Toward Unions, by FMCS Region
(percent affirmative responses)

Question	I.*	II.+	III.@	IV.#
Region:				
Eastern	85	12	88	21
Southern	94	24	94	12
Central	80	22	86	20
Western	65	4	96	4

*I. Unions should help troubled employers
+II. Unions are responsible for inflation
@III. Unions are responsible for American standard of living
#IV. Unions hinder the ability of American corporations to respond to international competition

Economic issues were important to mediators. Former union employees were more likely to attribute the high standard of living in the United States to union activities than were their colleagues (96% agreed as compared with 85%). Past

employment and agency affiliation had little influence, however, on whether mediators held unions
responsible for inflation, a proposal which mediators in 1985 denied slightly more strongly than
did their predecessors.

By 1985 the issue of union responsibility
for inflation had faded in importance in comparison with the problem of whether unions should
help companies which no longer could compete at
home or abroad. Mediators showed considerable
uncertainty about these two questions and expressed difficulty in understanding them. State
mediators, and especially those who usually
handled public sector disputes, revealed the
greatest indecision.

Federal mediators who concentrated on private
sector cases were more firmly convinced than were
their state colleagues who handled public sector
cases that unions did not hinder American productivity (76% and 53% respectively). FMCS staff
strongly (81%) believed that unions should make
concessions to help troubled companies, while one-
fourth of all public sector mediators were uncertain or failed to respond to this question (Figure 1).[6]

Thus mediators familiar with conditions in
the private sector tended to be sympathetic toward
unions, but they expected them to act responsibly.
They were more skeptical than their public sector
colleagues about managements' willingness to accept the unions' role in determining wages, hours
and working conditions.

Despite their belief in unions, the 1985
mediators showed somewhat less enthusiasm than did
their 1960s counterparts for the industrial relations system that developed under the NLRA. The
responses of both groups to all of the general
questions concerning collective bargaining issues
revealed less of a conviction that, in the words
of one mediator, "a free labor market is essential
and democratic." Instead, over one-fourth of the
respondents presumably agreed with their colleague
who denied that "the system will collapse without
collective bargaining."

FIGURE 1. <u>Attitudes Toward Unions, by Agency</u>
<u>and by Type of Cases</u>
(in percentages)

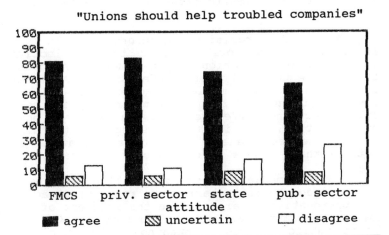

"Unions should help troubled companies"

This decline was more noticeable among state mediators. For example, in 1985 they were less convinced than were their predecessors that collective bargaining maintained industrial peace (agreement with this statement fell from 95% to 88%) and that it could resolve disputes between powerful opponents (84% in 1962 as compared with 71% in 1985). Among federal mediators, however, there was only a one or two percentage point shift over the quarter century.

Thus, the state mediators' attitudes toward the American industrial relations system changed more than those held by FMCS staff members. Presumably the growing difference in their background and in the legal context in which they worked increased the gap between their beliefs.

One example of how the different legal context in the public and private sector influenced attitudes toward collective bargaining issues was the question of whether mediation helps ensure industrial peace. By 1985 in the public sector

mediation was merely one step in the dispute
resolution process. Depending on local laws, this
process   might also include fact-finding and/or
one of several forms of arbitration. Failure to
settle a dispute through mediation was more likely
to lead to a lengthy quasi-judicial process with
limited economic implications for the parties than
to a strike.

It is not surprising, therefore, that in 1985
fewer state mediators believed that collective
bargaining and mediation helped to maintain industrial peace than did their predecessors. A higher
proportion of state mediators agreed that collective bargaining had been only moderately successful in settling differences between large and powerful parties. Nor is it surprising that the difference between federal and state mediators on
both of these issues increased over the years.

In 1985 mediators were more willing than were
their predecessors to narrow the range of managerial prerogative in areas where the interest of the
immediate community, rather than some vaguely defined public interest, appeared to be involved.
For example, in the 1960s only a slim majority of
all mediators believed that subcontracting and
plant relocation were suitable topics for bargaining. In 1985 more than two-thirds favored negotiating these issues although a few insisted that
both parties must agree to discuss them, and more
than 10% were undecided.

In two of the three questions involving managerial authority, FMCS mediators were more willing
to restrict the employers than were their state
colleagues. Attitudinal differences between
mediators who handled public and private sector
cases were smaller than those between state and
FMCS personnel on three of the five relevant questions. In both questions where type of cases
handled made a significant difference (whether employers should be required to provide financial
data and whether the introduction of technological
change was a suitable topic for collective bargaining), the difference can be attributed to the
large (over 10%) proportion of the state respondents who could not decide one way or another
(Table 2).

TABLE 2. <u>Scope of Bargaining: Managerial Rights</u>
(in percentages)

Question	Response	1962/64		1985	
		FMCS	State	FMCS	State
Must give	agree	48	36	73	71
financial	uncertain	11	9	5	9
information	disagree	41	55	22	20
percent difference			28		8
Should ne-	agree	40	32	25	20
gotiate	uncertain	10	13	10	16
technical	disagree	50	55	65	64
changes					
percent difference			16		12

Once again, differences among the responses from the four FMCS regions indicate the extent to which the mediators' attitudes on scope of bargaining issues were influenced by local economic conditions. Thus in 1985 (with the exception of disagreeing that the employers' right to subcontract unit work should be limited through collective bargaining) a majority of the Western FMCS respondents favored the widest possible scope for negotiations and unanimously agreed that collective bargaining was capable of resolving job security issues. Mediators in the Central Region, having experienced severe problems in the automotive and steel industries, were less optimistic about the ability of the negotiations system to resolve such problems (10% doubted it). In addition, relatively few (18% as compared with 38% of the Western respondents) believed that employers should be required to negotiate the introduction of technological change.

On the whole, prior employment experience exerted only a slight influence on the mediators' attitudes toward scope of bargaining issues. The

least enthusiasm (69% as compared with 75% overall) for negotiating plant relocation came from
mediators who had never worked for a union. One-
time managers were slightly less convinced than
were their nonmanagerial colleagues that job
security was a suitable subject for negotiation.
But union/management background had no noticeable
influence on whether mediators thought that controversies over subcontracting should be resolved
by collective bargaining, and on this question
state mediators were more willing than their FMCS
colleagues to limit managerial discretion. It
should be noted, however, that the differences between mediators on these issues was too small for
statistical significance.

Another issue upon which prior employment experience exerted an appreciable influence was the
previously discussed question of whether management must provide unions with financial data prior
to formal negotiations (Table 2). In the 1960s
45% of all mediators believed that management need
not do so, while in 1985 71% believed that they
should. As might be expected, former managers
were the least enthusiastic while mediators who
had had no supervisory or managerial experience
were the most likely to favor giving unions such
information (60% as compared with 79%, respectively).

Some of the change that occurred between the
1960s and 1985 in mediator beliefs concerning what
were appropriate subjects of bargaining might have
been due to judicial and NLRB rulings concerning
the duty to bargain. Thus, although the basic
court decisions that required employers to dis-
close relevant financial data date from the mid-
1950s, further clarification did not come until
1969 when the second circuit court issued its
ruling in General Electric v. NLRB.

Similarly, the Supreme Court decision that
companies must offer to negotiate before they
subcontract work performed by union members,
Fibreboard Paper Products Co. v. NLRB, appeared in
1964, too late to influence mediators' opinions in
the earlier survey; the fact that the case was
pending might have led to the high (16%) level of
"uncertain" responses among FMCS respondents that
year. Again, the Board's decision in 1966 to

apply <u>Fibreboard</u> to the problem of plant relocation came too late to affect mediator beliefs concerning the desirability of bargaining this
issue.

Where no relevant court or Board decision
existed or where the interests of the general
public did not appear to be directly affected,
mediators were reluctant to limit employer discretion. Moreover, they disagreed among themselves on issues where the relevant court decisions appeared to leave room for further interpretation.

The question of whether "the rate of introduction of technological change should be con-
trolled by collective bargaining" is an example of
such reluctance to restrict managerial rights. In
the 1960s 40% of the FMCS mediators believed that
technological innovations should be subject to negotiations, whereas in 1985 only one-fourth of
them agreed. Although there was no such decline
among state mediators, even former union members
showed little more enthusiasm than their non-union
colleagues for bargaining about new technology,
while mediators who at one time held a management
position rejected the proposal most strongly (by
70% as compared with 61% for those with no managerial experience). One state mediator pointed to
the solution common in the public sector where
management reserved the right to introduce new
technology, but its impact was subject to negotiations between labor and management.

<u>Conclusions: Attitudes in the 1960s and the 1980s</u>
Comparing the responses to a 1985 questionnaire with those collected a quarter century before, we can see that the attitudes of mediators
toward unions became more similar and more favorable during that time. Nonetheless, state mediators, who were less likely to have worked for a
union, expressed greater uncertainty on questions
concerning the economic impact of union activity.

The attitudes of state mediators toward the
American industrial relations system changed more
than those held by their FMCS colleagues. Both
groups were more willing in 1985 than were their

1960s counterparts to infringe on management prerogatives in areas affecting immediate community
interests.   Public sector mediators were more
likely to agree that mediators should serve the
public interest if "interest" was defined as
"maintaining productivity."   In addition, more
state than FMCS mediators accepted responsibility
for ensuring compliance with statutes and guidelines.

    Attitudes toward scope of bargaining issues
apparently were subject to a different set of influences.   FMCS respondents' reactions were also
influenced by regional economic conditions rather
than by agency affiliation.   Prior employment experience appeared to exert little influence.

    Some of the change in mediator attitudes
toward issues in collective bargaining, especially
the decline in the number of "uncertain" responses, can be attributed to judicial and NLRB
rulings between the 1960s and 1985 concerning the
duty to bargain.   In other cases, such as the
question of whether the introduction of technological change should be subject to negotiation,
nationwide economic developments evidently influenced mediator responses.

    On the whole, however, after reviewing
mediator attitudes toward the context in which
they functioned, we can conclude tentatively that
agency affiliation continued to exert a strong
influence on mediators, but that type of cases
handled played a role as well.   Education and
prior work experience evidently were considerably
less important, and, as indicated by a comparative
study of FMCS mediators by region, geographic
factors had only a narrow influence.

1. Thomas Kochan in New York State Public Employment Relations Bureau and New York State School of Industrial and Labor Relations at Cornell, <u>Symposium on Police and Firefighter Arbitration in New York State, December 1-3, 1976, Albany, New York</u>, p. 21 (hereafter, PERB). Kochan, et. al., "U.S. Industrial Relations System in Transition: A Summary Report," and responses by Ben Fischer, Jack Barbash, Janice McCormick and D. Quinn Mills, <u>Industrial Relations Research Association Proceedings of the 37th Annual Meeting, December 28-30, 1984, Dallas, Texas</u>, pp. 261-94. Peter Pestillio in SPIDR, 1982, p. 14.

2. Kolb linked her distinction between FMCS and state styles and strategies to the difference in type of cases that the two systems handled, and Arnold Zack, in his <u>Public Sector Mediation</u> (Washington, D.C.: Bureau of National Affairs, [1985]), cites her observations. Kolb's conclusions were, however, based on her experience in one state, and they do not necessarily apply in other areas of the country.

3. Interestingly enough, the percentage of FMCS mediators who had been union members or had served as union officers had increased from 73% and 53% in 1964 to 84% and 62% in 1985. On the other hand, the participation of state mediators declined: in 1962 78% had been union members and 47% had held union offices, while in 1985 the figures were 72% and 40%. Union membership declined with education: 91.2% of the mediators with a high school education only had, at one time, belonged to a union, while 71.4% of those who had attended college and 31.5% of those who went to graduate school reported union membership.

4. Seventy-three percent of the mediators who handled mostly private sector cases disagreed, as did 62% of those who dealt mainly with public sector cases.

5. As of February 1985, that is.

6. See Robert M. McKersie, "Putting the Ford-UAW Agreement and the Current Collective Bargaining

Scene in Perspective," in SPIDR, 1982, p. 22, for discussion of pressures on unions to make concessions.

7. 412 F.2d 512. The earlier decisions were <u>NLRB v. Truitt Manufacturing Co.</u>, 1956, 351 U.S. 149, 76 S.Ct. 753, 100 L.Ed. 1027; <u>NLRB v. F. W. Woolworth Co.</u>, 1956, 352 U.S. 938, 77 S.Ct. 261, 1 L.Ed. 2d 235.   Joel A. D'Alba discussed relevant state statutes and case law in "The Nature of the Duty to Bargain in Good Faith," in PERS, pp. 158-59.

8. <u>Ozark Trailers, Inc.</u>, 161 N.L.R.B. 561.

9. Arvid Anderson and Joan Weitzman, "The Scope of Bargaining in the Public Sector," PERS, pp. 178-79.

CHAPTER 6. MEDIATION AND THE
AMERICAN INDUSTRIAL RELATIONS SYSTEM

The opinions of the mediators who participated in the two surveys concerning the role that
their occupation plays in the American collective
bargaining system were influenced by their attitudes toward this system. These opinions were reflected in their responses to a number of questions which measured their dependence on the parties, the role that they attributed to strikes and
their beliefs concerning the impact of such procedures as fact-finding and arbitration.

In general, participants in both 1985 federal
and state surveys regarded the American industrial
relations system as an autonomous one which should
be kept as free as possible from outside interference. Nonetheless, differences existed in the degree to which they considered themselves to be
neutral facilitators or active participants in the
negotiation process. Based on their interpretation of their role in the collective bargaining
system, different mediators found varying tactics
and strategies to be appropriate.

In this and the following chapters we will
see whether their responses form a pattern. If
they do, we will try to determine the extent to
which they were influenced by such factors as
agency affiliation, prior employment experience
and regional economic environment.

Mediators somewhat grudgingly agreed (by 55%)
that the success of mediation depended on the
parties' attitudes, although federal mediators
were more convinced than their state colleagues
that they could, indeed, affect the outcome of
labor-management disputes; the difference between
the two groups on this issue increased over the
years.

Among FMCS mediators, those from the Eastern
Region were more convinced of their influence
(38% of the respondents believed that the success
of mediation depended on the parties' attitudes),
while 59% of the mediators from both the Southern
and Central Region agreed with that statement.

69

In other words, Eastern mediators had more confi-
dence in their ability to control the outcome
regardless of the parties' attitudes.

Over the years several observers noted a significant difference between FMCS and state agency
staff on the issue of mediator activism, or the
amount of influence they could and should exert on
the negotiating parties. This difference, supposedly, had led to divergent tactics and practices. In the immediate post-Taft-Hartley era,
they led to jurisdictional disputes between the
FMCS and state agencies which had largely disappeared by 1985. Some differences in practices
survived, however, and they will be discussed more
fully below.

How deep were the theoretical differences
between state and federal mediators, and to what
can they be attributed? During the 1950s rivalry
for cases was cited as the source. In the 1980s,
however, commentators claimed that state mediators
tended to favor more active intervention in the
negotiation process because their case load lay
primarily in the public sector where, in the words
of a student of mediation, Deborah Kolb, "the
ideology of free collective bargaining as it
exists in the private sector is anomalous in certain respects." FMCS director Kay McMurray explained that agency's continued (in 1981) adherence to the principles of voluntarism. According
to him:

> The current Administration is opposed
> to interference in the process of labor-
> management negotiations in the absence of
> a compelling national interest. Given
> the opportunities for agreement -- and
> disagreement -- the parties are free to
> chart their own economic and social
> course within the framework of tradi-
> tional industrial relations. We strongly
> believe that the marketplace will compel
> the parties to responsible and responsive
> agreements in the interest of labor, of
> management, and of the consumer -- and
> that is good for government.[2]

For others, however, the issue was more complex. Writing first in 1967 and again in 1977,

mediator and academician William M. Weinberg iden-
tified three types of state agencies: those which
believed mediation to be an extension of the collective bargaining   process, those which viewed
themselves as an arm of government functioning as
part of a broader regulatory system and those
which vacillated between the two positions.   How
an agency viewed itself, according to Weinberg,
influenced the way that its staff reacted to a
variety of issues including public responsibility,
the degree of active intervention which they found
appropriate and their ideas on when to intervene.
These differences, he argued in 1977, were inten-
sified, but not caused, by the degree to which an
agency concentrated on public sector cases.[3]

    In this and the following chapters we will
see the extent to which mediators accepted one
position or the other by analyzing their responses
to a series of questions concerning what they believed to be their primary responsibility.   Were
they more concerned with maintaining productivity,
with public or industrial interests, with achieving a settlement or a just settlement, and did
they regard themselves as responsible for ensuring
that all settlements in which they participated
observed statutory limitations?   In addition, we
will try to determine whether such divergences as
are noted between federal and state mediators on
issues related to the voluntary nature of collective bargaining can, indeed, be attributed to the
different nature of public and private sector collective bargaining.

    As noted in the previous chapter, mediators
regarded themselves as an integral part of a self-
governing industrial relations system.   What this
generalization means in practice is a frequently
discussed topic among academicians and practitioners.   Jeffrey B. Tener, the first full-time chairman of the New Jersey Public Employee Relations
Commission, summarized the position held by two-
thirds of the 1985 mediators: "The commitment of
the mediator is to the process, not any particular
outcome."[4]

    Others are less certain, however.   Arnold M.
Zack, a well-known independent mediator, posed a
problem that, despite Weinberg's typology, many
mediators hesitated to confront:

The question naturally arises whether the
mediator's primary duty is to serve the
public interest or to assist the parties.
This is particularly pertinent when one
considers that the "government" that may
provide the mediator in a public sector
dispute is also the employer. The issue
of divided loyalties is obvious.[5]

Some insist that mediators are responsible for
seeing that statutory limits on or executive
guidelines relating to collective bargaining are
respected by the negotiating parties. As collective bargaining spreads in public service and in
the health care industry, others believe that,
instead of maintaining a strict impartiality,
mediators should represent the interest of third
parties. Furthermore, the question arises as to
whether they can or should impose their own ideas
of equity and justice on the parties.[6]

According to their responses to the 1985 survey, at least 84% of all mediators believed that
gaining a settlement was more important than imposing their concept of equity (Table 1); as one
wrote, the "mediator should be alert for what will
settle, not be on an ideological crusade." This
was a notable increase over the approximately 70%
who took the same position in the 1960s.

Nonetheless, twice as many of the 1985
mediators accepted the proposition that mediators
serve the public interest when "interest" was specifically defined as "maintaining productivity"
than when it was left vague.[7] Mediators who
served in the public sector were considerably more
likely to accept such responsibility than were
those who usually handled private sector cases
(31.5% as compared with 18.5%).

Finally, although the proportion was still
large, 17% fewer of the state mediators disagreed
with the statement that they should be responsible
for ensuring compliance with statutes and guidelines than did FMCS mediators (88% of the federal
as compared with 71% of the state mediators).[8]

Thus, although the 1985 mediators supported
the general concept of a self-governing collec-

TABLE 1. <u>Mediator Responsibility, by Agency</u>
(in percentages)

Question	Response	FMCS	State
Serves public by maintaining productivity	agree	29	26
	?/blank	8	8
	disagree	63	66
	percentage difference*	6	
Serves public above parties	agree	17	12
	?/blank	2	9
	disagree	81	79
	percentage difference	14	
Settlement more important than equity	agree	84	86
	?/blank	3	6
	disagree	13	8
	percentage difference	10	
Responsible for statutes	agree	9	22
	?/blank	3	7
	disagree	88	71
	percentage difference	34	

*The sum of the difference between FMCS and state responses; the larger this figure is, the greater the difference is. When the responses were tabulated according to type of cases normally handled, the percentage differences were 26%, 4%, 4%, 24%, indicating that the only question upon which clientele exerted more influence on responses than agency affiliation was the first one.

tive bargaining system, more mediators in the state and public sector than in the federal, private sector were willing to impose some restrictions on the parties' freedom from outside inter-

ference. The difference between agencies on this
matter was greater than the difference between
public and private sector mediators.

The assumption that the collective bargaining
system is a self-governing one implies that the
parties have the right to decide when and if they
wish third party assistance in achieving their
labor contract. In the 1960s as well as in 1985
more than one-half of all mediators favored requiring parties to attempt mediation before engaging in a strike or lockout; the proportions
were virtually identical and did not change over
the intervening quarter century.

Three additional questions addressed the
issue of whether mediators could or should enter
negotiations regardless of the wishes of either
or both parties. In the 1960s and again in 1985
mediators responded to these questions in a consistent, albeit a lackluster, fashion. The difference diminished between FMCS and state responses to all three questions. For example, one-
third or more of the FMCS respondents to the first
survey were willing to intervene without the approval of one or both of the parties, while only
one-fourth of the state mediators were willing to
do so. By 1985 there was no significant difference between state and federal mediators on this
issue; more than 60% agreed that the parties'
wishes should be respected.

Classifying responses according to type of
cases normally handled reveals that public sector
mediators had the same regard for the parties'
autonomy as had their private sector colleagues.
In fact, the state mediators' increasing concentration on public sector disputes did not reduce
their respect for the voluntary nature of mediation. Instead, in the 1985 survey private-sector
oriented federal mediators agreed with their
state colleagues that "the continued effectiveness of a mediator depends upon his not intruding
himself when or where he is not wanted" with
almost the same degree of enthusiasm, a somewhat
tepid 64%.[9]

Mediators applied their ideas about voluntarism fairly consistently, although they demonstrated less uniformity on the issue of whether

public sector and health care negotiations required special restrictions on the right to
strike.   This is significant because a major
practical distinction between public and private
sector is whether the parties are permitted to
resort to economic coercion -- either strikes or
lockouts.[10]   State and federal mediators differed
as to whether they believed that the pressure of a
possible strike was necessary for successful collective bargaining and what alternatives should be
offered in the public sector.

Public opinion tends to regard all strikes as
avoidable evils.   In the euphoria that followed
World War II, Americans assumed that industrial
peace was an absolute goal toward which all efforts should be directed, a belief which the lan-
guage of the Wagner and the Taft-Hartley Acts appeared to confirm.[11]   During the 1950s some
writers began to question whether our society
really believed that industrial peace was possible, or, indeed, desirable, and by the 1960s some
psychologists and industrial relations practitioners argued that conflict could not or should not
always be avoided.

Even so, over the years public tolerance for
industrial conflict diminished, and pessimists oc-
casionally warned that, unless mediators represented the public interest, Congress would amend
the labor act to impose on all collective bargaining restrictions on the right to strike similar to
those contained in the 1974 health care amendments.[12]

Mediator attitudes toward the role that
strikes play in the collective bargaining process
were somewhat less consistent than was their respect for the parties' autonomy.   Over 90% of all
mediators believed that mediation did, in fact,
reduce strikes.   Although a majority of all respondents agreed that either the threat or the
actuality of a strike could serve a useful purpose, federal mediators were more likely to accept
the possibility of industrial conflict than were
state mediators.

Comparing FMCS responses on the only related
question that was reported in the 1960s, more
mediators believed in 1985 than in 1964 that nego-

tiations required "the pressure of contract expiration" and, implicitly of a strike."[13]   Although 68% of the mediators who usually handled
public sector cases agreed that a strike might
serve to clear the air, barely half of them believed that laws which prohibited strikes by government employees hindered collective bargaining.
As one commented, "Pressure is still there even in
the form of illegal action."   There is little
reason therefore, to attribute the federal mediators' increased appreciation of the role played by
strike threats to their experience with the frequently protracted public sector negotiations.

Consistent with their belief that mediation
helped to prevent strikes, a bare majority of the
1985 mediators, as well as those in the 1960s,
permitted their desire to promote industrial peace
to temper their respect for the voluntary nature
of collective bargaining.   Thus 52% of participating FMCS mediators, both in 1964 and in 1985,
believed that "legislation should require the parties to utilize mediation before a strike can
legally begin."

But familiarity with such laws did not auto-
matically lead to enthusiasm for them; although
almost all state public sector labor laws require
mediation, even in the few jurisdictions that permit strikes, only 63% of the responding state
mediators approved of them.   This represents a
mere 2% increase over the figure in 1962 when very
few mediators had had any experience with mandatory dispute settlement procedures.

In their efforts to avoid strikes, many
states developed such forms of third-party intervention as fact-finding and interest arbitration.
These procedures have been discussed extensively
in the literature, and observers disagree about
their effectiveness.   In general, unions that
represent employees in states that forbid public
sector strikes have favored their implementation.
At least initially, spokesmen for school boards
and municipal officials objected to them, arguing
that they infringed on the responsibility of
elected government officials, increased the size
of settlements and discouraged the parties from
reaching their own agreements.[14]

Mediators are not concerned with the first
two arguments although several studies have attempted to substantiate or refute them.[15] But
mediators expressed concern about the impact of
binding arbitration and fact-finding on their role
in the dispute settlement process (Table 2). Interestingly, FMCS respondents demonstrated the
greatest hostility toward compulsory arbitration.
Although, presumably, state mediators have had
more experience with such practices, the federal
mediators were more convinced that it chilled
mediation in the public sector and (in the area
where perhaps they had greater familiarity) denied
that it should be used for contract negotiations
in the health care industry. For their part,
mediators who generally handled public sector disputes and who had the most experience with fact-
finding and interest arbitration were less certain
about their effects. While 48% agreed that they

TABLE 2. <u>Attitudes toward Compulsory Arbitration</u>,
<u>by Agency</u>
(in percentages)

Question	Response	FMCS		State
It chills	agree	77		48
mediation in	?/blank	9		10
the public	disagree	14		42
sector				
	percentage difference		58	
Should use	agree	30		30
for public	?/blank	10		14
sector	disagree	60		56
	percentage difference		8	
Should use	agree	28		46
for health	?/blank	6		14
care cases	disagree	66		40
	percentage difference		52	

---

discouraged serious negotiation, 42% disagreed and the remaining 10% were undecided.

Only the responses to the question of whether all collective bargaining should be subject to compulsory arbitration were reported in the 1960s. At that time well over 95% of both the federal and state mediators thought that it should not be. By 1985, however, the percentage of state mediators who opposed mandatory arbitration had fallen to 81%; 13% thought that it should be required and 6% were uncertain.

Classifying the responses by public and private sector clientele, mediators who handled public sector cases were somewhat more likely to accept the general concept of compulsory arbitration (13%) than those whose experience lay primarily in the private sector (4%). Interestingly enough, neither union affiliation nor management experience had a significant effect on attitudes toward this question. Close to one-third of the 1985 respondents believed that compulsory arbitration was appropriate for the public sector; there was no significant difference between federal and state, public and private sector mediators on this issue.

Some respondents, however, excluded police and fire negotiations from their opposition to compulsory arbitration. Health care was still another area where mediators were willing to require interest arbitration.[16] State and federal mediators differed significantly on this issue, however. While almost half of the state respondents agreed that compulsory arbitration was necessary, this opinion was shared by less than one-third of the FMCS mediators, who handled a larger percentage of all health care cases.

It might be concluded, therefore, that in 1985 mediators still did not like alternate forms of third-party intervention in the collective bargaining process, and that those at the state level, where fact-finding and interest arbitration were common, tended to view it with the greatest skepticism. There is insufficient evidence to determine whether FMCS hesitancy concerning compulsory arbitration for health care cases was a

result of bad experience with boards of inquiry
established by the 1974 amendments or whether it
reflected the above-quoted administrative policy
concerning voluntarism.[17]

1. Zack, p. 181, says that the realization that the parties' attitudes are decisive comes with experience; see Kochan, p. 279. In addition to being more skeptical about their ability to influence disputes, state mediators expressed a high (14%) degree of uncertainty. Analyzing by types of cases handled did not increase the difference.

2. McMurray, p. 70; Kolb, p. 157. For earlier discussions see Weisenfeld, Mediation, and Weinberg, "An Administrative History." We will discuss this difference in greater detail below. Several FMCS respondents thought that the Service should not handle public sector disputes. When this issue arose in the mid-1970s, the FMCS defended its jurisdiction on the grounds that state mediation facilities frequently were inadequate; Herbert Fishgold, pp. 731-37.

3. Weinberg, "Bureaucratic Expediency" and "Ethical Questions Confronting the Mediator," presented to SPIDR, Oct. 24, 1977, condensed in SPIDR, 1977 Proceedings, Fifth Annual Meeting,Oct. 23-26, 1977.

4. Tener, "Mediator Skills," SPIDR, 1982, p. 65.

5. Zack, p. 10. In his response to the 1985 survey, one mediator noted the difficulties engendered by his status as a government employee. Tener's position was shared by such other state agency administrators as Harold R. Newman (in PERS, p. 196). According to Don S. Wasserman, The American Federation of Federal, State, County and Municipal Employees has long questioned the involvement of government employees in their disputes with state governments; "A Union View of the Neutral," SPIDR, 1982, p. 47.

6. Joseph B. Stulberg citing Larry Susskind, in SPIDR, 1982, p. 38; Walter J. Gershenfeld, "Public Employee Unionization -- An Overview," in PERS, pp. 17-18, Kochan, pp. 280 and 285; and William E. Simkin, Mediation and the Dynamics of Collective Bargaining (Washington, D.C.: Bureau

of National Affairs, 1971), pp. 34-40; Weinberg, "Bureaucratic" and "Ethics."

7. In checking his opposition to the more limited statement, one federal mediator quipped, "Take that, Larry Susskind."

8. Stulberg, a professor at the City University of New York's Baruch College, argues that mediators are bound by the law and thus are limited in the kind of issues they should permit parties to address through mediation; "A Mediator's Neutrality: Fact or Fiction?" SPIDR, 1982, p. 37.

9. Analysis by types of cases normally handled revealed even less difference between mediators.

10. There are, of course, a wide variety of other important differences which are summarized in Gershenfeld (PERS, pp. 12-15) and Zack. This difference may disappear if the trend in the private sector toward a reduced reliance on strike threats continues and if Gershenfeld is correct in concluding that opposition to public sector strikes is diminishing (PERS, p. 19 and Bureau of Labor Statistics' July 1985 report on major work stoppages).

11. For example, Elmore Jackson, Meeting of Minds: A Way to Peace through Mediation (New York: McGraw-Hill, Inc., 1952), p. 5; Edward Peters, Conciliation in Action: Principles and Techniques (New London, Conn.: National Foremen's Institute, [1952]), pp. 21-22; Wagner Act, sec. 1, and LMRA, 1 (b). See also Ken Moffett in The Public Interest and the Role of the Neutral in Dispute Settlement: Proceedings of the Inaugural Convention of the Society of Professionals in Dispute Resolution, Reston, Va., October 17-19, 1973 (hereafter SPIDR, 1973), p. 21. George Taylor, Government Regulation of Industrial Relations.

12. Kochan discusses this issue (pp. 236-38), citing, among others, Abe Raskin of The New York Times on the need to limit the right to strike. See also SPIDR, 1980, p. 24; James Mackranz, "General Role of Mediation in Collective Bargaining," Labor Law Journal, June, 1960, p. 454.

From time to time Congress, as well as various
state legislatures, has enacted laws designed to
settle specific strikes regarded as contrary to
the public interest.

13. Indik, p. 28.   The question was not asked on
the state form.   Unfortunately, the original 1960s
data cannot be located.   Several respondents commented that the wording of the question made it
difficult to answer.   See also Kochan, p. 278.

14. As of spring 1985 only eleven states gave
public employees at least a limited right to
strike.   A classic example of the school boards'
position is given in David R. Friedman and Stuart
S. Mukamal, "Wisconsin's Mediation-Arbitration
Law: What Has It Done to Bargaining?" Journal of
Collective Negotiations in the Public Sector, 13
(1984): 171-89.   The authors conclude that "the
inevitable result is the displacement of real bargaining by litigation."   Summary of recent studies
in Kochan, p. 278, n. 6, and 279.   The director of
the New York State Office of Employee Relations,
Donald H. Wollett, quoted George Taylor to the
effect that "compulsory arbitration is a greater
threat [than strikes among public employees].   It
entails the delegation to outsiders of the authority assigned by the electorate to elected officials who are subject to the checks and balances
of our governmental institutions"; NYS PERB, p.
129.

15. Kochan's study summarized in NYS PERB; reports
in NYS PERB; reports in ALRA proceedings for 1983
and 1984; publications by Bloom and Ashenfelter
listed in bibliography; Richard A. Lester, Labor
Arbitration in State and Local Government: An
Examination of Experience in Eight States and New
York City (Princeton, N.J.: Industrial Relations
Section, Dept. of Economics, [1984]); Raymond L.
Hogler and Curt Kriksciun, "Impasse Resolution in
Public Sector Collective Negotiations: A Proposed
Procedure," Industrial Relations Law Journal 6,
(1984): 481-510; James L. Stern, Charles M.
Rehmus, et. al., Final-Offer Arbitration (Lexing-
ton, Mass.: Lexington Books, 1975).

16. In several states mandatory arbitration
applied only to police and fire disputes or to

those defined as involving "essential services."

17. Evidently, such boards have proven unsatisfactory and rarely are appointed.   See the discussions in Ira Michael Shepard and A. Edward Doudera, <u>Health Care Labor Law</u> (Ann Arbor, Mich.: Association of University Programs in Health Administration Press, 1981).   The FMCS interpreted the 1977 amendments to the NLRA as giving them jurisdiction over all health care cases, although in 1985 62% of the participating state mediators reported that they had handled some cases during the preceding year.

CHAPTER 7. PROFESSIONAL ISSUES IN MEDIATION

The Mediator's Job: Status, Recognition and Other Issues

In 1985 mediators believed that the public at large did not appreciate the importance of their role, although over 90% believed that unions and, to a lesser extent (70%)[1], managers recognized the need for their services. Within the FMCS Eastern mediators were most dubious about management willingness to accept mediation (62% thought that they did), while 80% of the mediators from the Central Region thought that managements favored mediation.

Thus one FMCS mediator expressed a liking for public sector cases on the grounds that they publicized the mediation process. This attitude, if widely held, would explain why slightly fewer mediators who worked in the public sector regarded themselves as unappreciated than did private sector mediators (67% and 72%, respectively; the difference between state and FMCS responses was smaller -- 70% and 72%, respectively).

In the 1960s both state and federal mediators thought that the parties used mediation as a way to avoid direct negotiations. In 1985 both groups disagreed, although the proportion of federal mediators who rejected this statement was considerably (19%) greater. It might be argued that this difference reflected a continuing tendency among less experienced public employers and unions to use mediation in order to achieve goals that they could not win at the bargaining table. However, there actually was less of a difference on this question between public and private sector mediators than between state and FMCS staff (38% as compared with 28% total difference).[2]

Another significant factor might be the familiarity with and respect mediators for private sector management and union spokesmen. The officials who negotiated for public employers and, to a lesser extent, the unions that represented government workers were not yet "pros" by 1985, and mediators found it more difficult to work with them.[3] These reactions may contribute to the feeling that employers and unions do not appreciate their efforts.

As happens with an occupation that regards itself as unappreciated, mediators developed a mystique concerning their work. Three-fourths of the respondents were convinced that mediation did, indeed, influence the outcome of the disputes in which they intervened, while 90% believed that their efforts reduced the number of strikes. They were firmly convinced that mediation was an art which could not be taught, and they were devout generalists. Although they were interested in professionalism and believed that their ability could be measured, they differed among themselves on a variety of professional issues.

One area in which they differed significantly was mediator-client relationships. State mediators expressed less certainty about the nature of the mediator-client relationship than did their federal colleagues. There are two possible and perhaps connected explanations; FMCS mediators tended to be more comfortable with their clients, and operational differences among the agencies made some matters more important for federal than for state mediators.

Two questions measured mediator attitudes toward their relationships with their clients. On the issue of whether a neutral should follow a case if the site changed (Figure 1), 70% of the FMCS respondents agreed, while one-fourth of the state mediators either were uncertain or did not answer the question (62% agreed, however). State cases were less likely to move, and it was easier for the mediators to follow if they did move. On the other hand, the issue of moving with a case became more significant for federal mediators because, under the reorganization of the early 1980s although the FMCS districts increased in size, travel funds were curtailed. It became increasingly difficult for the federal mediator to follow if, for some reason or other, parties in a multiplant operation decided to shift negotiations to another location.

Participants were also asked whether the same mediator should assist if the parties needed help in resolving subsequent labor disputes (Figure 2).

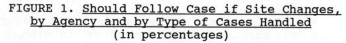

FIGURE 1. Should Follow Case if Site Changes,
    by Agency and by Type of Cases Handled
              (in percentages)

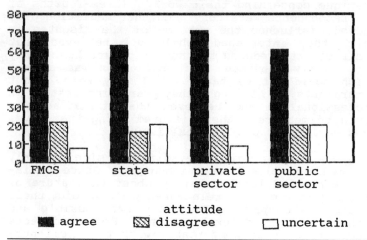

Twenty-two percent of the state mediators were uncertain, and mediators who handled public sector
cases expressed even greater indecision (25%). On
the other hand, more than half of the federal
mediators believed that continuity was an
advantage, a response which possibly reflected
their better relationships with their clients.

      There were differences within the FMCS,
however. The Eastern mediators were more likely to
think that they should assist the same clients in
subsequent disputes (74% as compared with 39% of
their Western colleagues). A higher percentage
(75%) of the Western mediators believed that they
should follow a case if the site of negotiations
changed, while only 59% of the Southern staff
agreed. Keeping in mind that the Eastern mediators
found their client relationships to be more
satisfactory than did Westerners, it was not surprising that the former would be more interested in
establishing a long-term relationship, even though
they did not feel as strongly about retaining
jurisdiction over cases.

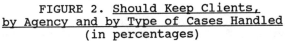

FIGURE 2. Should Keep Clients,
by Agency and by Type of Cases Handled
(in percentages)

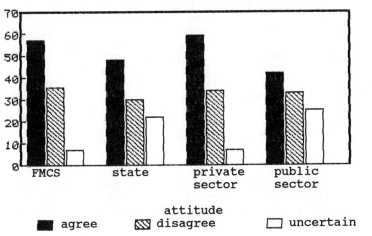

In general, most of the federal mediators had a clearer picture of and more firmly established beliefs concerning their occupation than did their counterparts in state agencies. For example, on an issue which, perhaps, is tangentially related to client relationships, the question of whether mediators should specialize, federal mediators were almost unanimous (91% disapproved) while a relatively high percentage (17%) of the state respondents were undecided.

The majority of the respondents, either state or FMCS, believed that solo full-time staff mediators provided better assistance than either ad hoc or panel mediation. Traditionally, agency mediaors have viewed part-time practitioners skeptically, except perhaps for a few "superstars" who either have a standing relationship with a particular industry or have clearly demonstrated their labor relations expertise in another area. Even then agency staff fear that their "halo" will overshadow the work performed by full-time neutrals. Self-employed mediators are less concerned with agency responsibility than are staff members, and some

fear that ad hoc practitioners will be unable to
respond to sudden demands for their services.[4]

In their responses to the 1985 survey, mediators expressed less certainty and perhaps less
concern about ad hoc or panel mediation than did
their earlier counterparts; "undecided" responses
on the five questions related to ad hoc, dual and
panel mediation were as high as 44% (i.e., public
sector mediators on the statement that dual mediation is satisfactory from the parties' point of
view).[5]   On all related questions, state/public
mediators had less firm opinions than did their
federal colleagues, even when asked about ad hoc or
part-time mediators, the use of which was more
common in the public than in the private sector.

Federal mediators were also ambivalent toward
ad hoc practitioners (16% "undecided" responses).
In addition, they disliked dual mediation (74%
denied that it was satisfactory for the parties
and 77% regarded it as unsatisfactory for mediators).

The Central Region was the most strongly opposed (86%) to dual mediation, while Southern
mediators were least opposed (68%).   This difference is attributable to local conditions in that
there were virtually no state mediation agencies
with competing jurisdiction in the Southern Region
as there were in the East (where 82% of the respondents found dual mediation to be unsatisfactory).
Nonetheless, although there were some well established state labor relations agencies in the Central Region, in Ohio and Illinois they were in the
process of being established in early 1985 when the
survey was conducted.   Perhaps some of the respondents in the Central Region were reacting to a potential rather than an actual situation.

One federal mediator felt so strongly about
dual mediation that he wrote a lengthy note in
which he itemized what he considered to be its
"important problems."   They were:

    1. Obviously not cost-effective
    2. Tendency of parties to feel one media-
       tor is management[']s mediator, other
       [is] union['s].
    3. Lack of confidentiality and violation of

        code of professional conduct
    4. Problem of who will call shots when
       there is no time for a caucus between
       mediators
    5. Scheduling difficulties.
    6. Turf problems
        a. state agencies['] feeling they have
           a right to "a presence" at the
           table even in health care cases.
        b. grabbing any case that comes along
           when you know it should be handled
           by another agency.
        c. private mediators "offering their
           services" during a strike.

A state mediator who, himself, had no personal
experience with dual mediation reported that his
colleagues not only disliked it and regarded it as
a waste of resources, but that they "view it as a
bureaucratic device for preserving staff." State
and federal mediators also expressed negative
attitudes toward panel mediation.[6]

    A special form of panel mediation occurs in
the FMCS where in important cases representatives
from the national office assist field staff. This
issue was touched upon in the earlier discussion
of job satisfaction (Chapter 4, pp. 52-53). Judg-
ing by their responses, the eight participating
federal mediators who handled public sector cases
were more defensive about their relationship with
representatives of the national office than were
the 144 FMCS respondents who usually mediated
private sector disputes. Despite such comments as
"they often interfere or 'run over' local mediators," three-fourths of all FMCS respondents
claimed to find national help useful. Even so,
only 31% of them were willing to let the National
Office representative chair mediation panels.

Mediation Strategy and Tactics
    Some observers believe that Kolb's char-
acterization of state agency employees as
dealmakers and FMCS staff as orchestrators high-
lights the most important distinctions among
mediators. Looking at various tactics, we will
see whether the extent to which participants in
the 1985 survey favored a passive or an active
role depended on agency affiliation or on other

factors.   It may well be, as Massachusetts Institute of Technology professor Thomas A. Kochan in-
sists, that passivity is more suited to early
stages in mediation and that mediators take an
increasingly active part as contract expiration
approaches.   Unfortunately, the current survey
does not permit us to test this assertion.   The
responses are difficult to interpret because,
fearing client criticism and firmly committed to
the voluntary nature of collective bargaining,
some mediators might have been reluctant to assert
that they made a substantive contribution to the
negotiation process.

Mediators describe themselves as catalysts.
They define their tasks as providing technical
services, supplying skills that the parties lack,
serving as repositories for information, clarify-
ing and narrowing issues, offering "reality in-
put," acting as a bridge between parties, and
transmitting outside pressures.   Most importantly,
they act as "lightning rods," making an unpopular
settlement possible by serving as fall guys and
permitting negotiators to save face with their
constituencies.

Disagreement concerning the mediators' responsibility and the degree to which they should
take an active part in settling disputes has encouraged industrial relations practitioners and
behavioral scientists to take a closer look at the
mediation process.   Studies dating from the 1950s
and 1960s proved unsatisfactory because behavioral
scientists frequently were unfamiliar with industrial relations and made assumptions or established
goals that practitioners rejected.   On the other
hand, mediators tend to be pragmatic and "atheoretical."   Their conviction that mediation is an art
and is highly idiosyncratic makes generalization
practically impossible, and they tend to distrust
the findings of academicians who study their work.
Presumably this hostility will diminish as the proportion of mediators who have attended graduate
school increases.

In 1985, even more than in the 1960s, mediators believed that it was better to be forceful
than to be timid; as one noted, "I've never known a
'timid' mediator."   They did not believe themselves
to be bound by the parties to the dispute and in-

sisted that rather than merely transmitting proposals they should evaluate the suggestions on the
basis of external, objective standards. They
favored manipulation or creation of deadlines and
universally agreed that they should propose alternate solutions for the parties' consideration.[10]

In response to specific questions, in 1985
both state and federal mediators believed that they
need not reflect the party's relative strength when
they transmitted proposals to the other side. This
is an example of an issue upon which the attitudes
of both groups have converged over the years; in
the 1960s there was a 34% difference between the
two which by 1985 had declined to 18%.

The attitudes of state and federal mediators
were closer, although they were ambivalent, on the
question of whether it was better to let the
parties exert their own pressure face-to-face
rather than have the mediator serve as a conduit
(44% agreed, 48% disagreed and 8% were undecided).
Computing responses according to type of cases
normally handled shows that public sector mediators
saw less value in having the parties exert direct
pressure than did private sector mediators.

Although mediators had mixed feelings about
whether they should play the "devil's advocate" in
separate meetings -- 52% of the state mediators
agreed, as did 41% of the FMCS -- 86% denied that
they should "aggressively support the position of
one side or the other" in joint conferences.

Similarly, federal mediators were ambivalent
as to whether they should publish their recommendations in order to exert pressure on the parties,
while a bare majority of their state colleagues
rejected the proposition. All mediators agreed
that they should deflate extreme stands; distinctions between state and federal, public and private sector were insignificant, and the proportion
of positive responses was the same in the 1960s
and in 1985.

In 1964 FMCS respondents felt less bound by
the parties; three-quarters of them thought that
it was permissible to assume an advocate's role in
a separate meeting, a majority thought that they
should publish recommendations under certain

circumstances, and somewhat more of them than in
1985 (although by no means a majority) believed
that they might support one side or the other in a
joint meeting.   Unfortunately, state mediators
were not asked these questions in 1962.

Practicing mediators agreed with scholars
that their discretion should be tempered by the
need to respect confidential information.[11] They
also believed that they should clear proposals
with both parties before making a recommendation
at a joint session -- the proportion of federal
mediators agreeing with this statement did not
change between 1964 and 1985, while state mediators were less certain than their federal colleagues (56% as compared with 68%).

Another important tactic used by mediators is
the manipulation of separate and joint meetings,[12]
and in 1985, even more than in the 1960s, the respondents disagreed with the proposition that they
should separate the parties only when progress appeared possible (by eight percentage points for
federal and by nine points for state mediators).
One respondent bluntly commented that the
"questioner does not understand the process,"
another argued that "separate caucuses give each
side a chance to rethink," while Tener insisted
that separate meetings provided mediators with an
opportunity to force parties to be realistic.[13]

Mediators were asked when they believed to be
the best time to enter a dispute (Table 1).   The
question is considered significant because at one
time critics of the federal service claimed that
jurisdictional rivalry[14] led FMCS mediators to
intervene prematurely.   The 1985 responses
indicated a trend toward earlier entry among FMCS
staff.   Although the percentage of those favoring
an earlier entrance declined from 5% to 1% (and
that 1% consisted of mediators from the Southern
Region), the proportion favoring entering when
"well underway" as opposed to "at impasse" rose
from 49% to 60%.   Within the FMCS, the Southern
mediators preferred to enter earlier than their
colleagues (3% chose "early," 68% "well underway"
and 29% "at impasse"), while those from the Central
Region advocated waiting the longest (55% selected
"well underway" and 45% "at impasse").

TABLE 1. When Prefer to Enter Disputes,
by Agency, 1960s and 1985
(in percentages)

when prefer	1962/64 FMCS	1962/64 state	1985 FMCS	1985 state
early	5	13	1	2
well underway	49	18	60	24
impasse	46	69	36	73

A similar trend can be observed among state mediators, although, as noted earlier, a regional breakdown of responses could not be made. Between 1962 and 1985 the percentage of those favoring early entry declined from 13% to 2%. More of the 11% difference opted for entrance "when well underway" (6%) than for "at impasse" (4%). Thus the direction of change was the same for both FMCS and state mediators, but the difference between the two groups on this issue increased (from 62% to 77%) over the twenty-five years between the two studies.

In order to measure the difference between theory and practice, mediators were asked at what stage they had actually entered negotiations during the previous year. Responses to this question were difficult to interpret, and their accuracy is questionable. Nonetheless, they do indicate that the average stage for the federal mediator was "well underway" while for state mediators it was "impasse." Unlike 1964, when federal mediators reported that, although they would have liked to have entered earlier, they most frequently entered negotiations at impasse, by 1985 they were able to match practice with theory and more frequently entered disputes at the "well underway" stage.

Mediators were asked to rank a list of tactics according to effectiveness in achieving settlements. These tactics were: appealing to mutual consent of the parties, to the mutual benefits of settling, to the mediators' status as

experts, to their status as representatives of
the public, and to their image as boss.

    Despite the insistence of several respondents
that they selected methods according to circumstances and presumably to the stage that negotiations had reached, their replies showed a clear
pattern (Table 2). All mediators agreed on rank
order, and 93% regarded the "boss" approach as
least effective. A majority also agreed that ex-
ploiting their status as representatives of the
public interest accomplished little. There was
less agreement, however, about which tactics were
useful. More (49%) selected an appeal to mutual
interests as the best method, but only a third
agreed on how they would rate "benefit of settlement" and using the mediator's status as an expert.

TABLE 2. Settlement Tactics, by Agency

appeal to:	rank	percent place in this rank	
		FMCS	state
mutual consent	1	52	44
benefit of settlement	2	40	35
status as expert	3	34	30
status as public representative	4	64	72
status as boss	5	97	90

    There was greater agreement among federal
mediators as to how they evaluated these tactics
than among their state colleagues. The distinction between whether the respondent normally
handled public or private sector cases was significant in how they viewed only two items; considerably more (17%) mediators who handled private
than public sector cases believed that appealing
to mutual consent was an effective way to end a
dispute, while slightly more private than public
sector mediators regarded an appeal to the media-

tor's expert status as a useful ploy (33% as compared with 27%; the average was 30%).

Conclusions: Professional Attitudes over a Quarter Century

In 1985 many mediators believed that the public at large did not appreciate their services,
although they thought that their clients respected
them.   FMCS staff tended to feel more comfortable
with the parties to a dispute and were somewhat
more likely to favor the establishment of long-run
relationships between client and mediator than
were their state colleagues.

In the 1985 survey, federal and state mediators differed even more than they had in the 1960s
on the extent to which they believed that their
efforts affected the outcome of labor management
disputes.   Although state mediators were more
familiar with mandatory mediation, binding arbitration and fact-finding, they found these to be
less desirable procedures than did federal mediators.   FMCS personnel, on the other hand, viewed
strikes in a more positive light than did their
state colleagues.

Federal mediators had better defined attitudes toward their profession, its strategy and
its tactics.   Although their practice of entering
disputes earlier than their state colleagues had
increased in the last two decades, this did not
necessarily mean that federal mediators advocated
more forceful or "bossy" tactics.[15]   Differences
between the two groups concerning whether they
should enter disputes without the approval of one
or both of the parties largely disappeared in the
interval between the two surveys.   Moreover, all
mediators agreed in identifying tactics which did
not help settle disputes.   But there was greater
agreement among FMCS personnel than among state
mediators as to the rank order of a given group of
tactics.

Mediators within the FMCS showed a remarkable
degree of agreement when their attitudes toward
professional questions were analyzed by region
despite certain differences which can be attributed to local economic factors.   This reinforces

the evidence which will be discussed further in
the next chapter that agency affiliation rather
than education, prior work experience or age
exerted the strongest influence on mediators.

On the basis of their responses to specific
questions, we can furthermore see that state and
federal mediators did not neatly sort themselves
into "dealmakers" and "orchestrators." Although
some differences can be discerned in both the
theory and practice of when they should enter disputes, the image of the federal mediator who
gently coaxes the parties to agreement as con-
trasted with the state mediator who sweats through
the process, pushing and pulling his clients
along, does not coincide with the mediators' self-
concept. Such differences as existed lay in a
greater certainty on the part of the FMCS mediators concerning various professional issues and
the greater ease that they felt in dealing with
their clients.

On the whole, despite the increasing divergence in types of cases handled and prior work
experience between federal and state mediators,
their disagreements concerning strategy and tactics diminished over the years. Thus in practice,
if not in theory, the 1985 mediators believed that
public sector collective bargaining did not really
require a new approach on the part of the neutrals
who handled conflicts between governments and
their employees. We will now investigate whether
a deeper analysis of the responses to the 1985
survey can provide us with a better understanding
of the extent to which demographic characteristics
and prior experience influenced mediator attitudes.

1. The 1960s responses to these questions were not reported. Zack attributed the lack of public appreciation to a paucity of up-to-date literature concerning mediation; see his introduction. Most recent publications focus on the public sector: Kochan, p. 272 ff.

2. There also was little difference between mediators in their response to the proposition that the use of mediation is a sign of the parties' immaturity -- 90% of all respondents rejected this statement.

3. Commentators disagree concerning the extent to which this difference in sophistication persisted into the 1980s. Zack (p. 16) found that it continued to be a significant factor, while Gershenfeld (PERS, p. 12) believed it to be a diminishing problem. Kolb, p. 156, discussed the relationship between mediators and pros. See GERR, Jan. 21, 1980, 845: 18 for a warning against "excessive use" of neutrals which, supposedly, has a "narcotic effect on negotiations." Norman Metzger, an authority on collective bargaining in the health care industry, says that this has been true in past hospital negotiations, while Zack also found that public sector negotiators tended to use mediation as a substitute for direct bargaining (p. 5).

4. Simkin, 122-23 and 352; Robins and Denenberg, pp. 9-10; Zack, pp. 20-21. Individual mediators who were interviewed in 1983 for a preliminary study regarded this as a dead issue. According to them, most part-time mediators were local arbitrators who had previously worked with the parties.

5. The five statements held that: dual mediation is unsatisfactory for mediators; dual mediation is satisfactory for parties; ad hoc mediation is not useful; panels should not be established without a recommendation by the mediator; and panels reduce the mediators' status. The 1962 state questionnaire did not include any of these questions, and FMCS responses were reported for only the first two.

6. For an early statement based on Connecticut's experience, see Robert L. Stutz, "Troikas, Duets and Prima Donnas in Labor Mediation," Labor Law Journal, Oct. 1962, pp. 845-52. See also Simkin, pp. 161 and 126.

7. Kochan, pp. 279-83. He notes that some parties have become suspicious of mediation tactics; comments by Ben Fischer, David Cole and Douglas Soutar in SPIDR, 1973, pp. 106-108, 56-57 and 121-22; see also arch-critic Herbert R. Northrup's "Mediation -- the Viewpoint of the Mediated," Labor Law Journal, (Oct. 1962), p. 833.

8. Discussions with practitioners; Simkin; Robins and Schneider; Zack; Peters, Conciliation; Peters, "The Mediator: A Neutral, a Catalyst, or a Leader," Labor Law Journal (Oct. 1958), pp. 764-65; Walter A. Maggiolo, Techniques of Mediation in Labor Disputes (Dobbs Ferry, N.Y.: Oceana, 1971); Paul Yager, "Mediation: A Conflict Resolution Technique in the Industrial Community and Public Sectors," New Techniques in Labor Dispute Resolution: A Report of the 23 Conference of the ALMA (July 28-Aug. 2, 1974) and the 2nd Conference of the SPIDR, Nov. 11-13, 1974 (Washington, D.C.: BNA, 1976), p. 126. Roger Fisher and William Ury, Getting to Yes: Negotiating Agreement Without Giving In (Boston: Houghton Mifflin Co., [1981]).

9. Peters, Conciliation, pp. 147-48; Allan Weisenfeld, "Profile," p. 872; Moffet in SPIDR, 1973, p. 21. Kochan reviewed some additional studies, pp. 239-48. Surveys are subject to less criticism although some mediators have privately said that the right questions are never asked. For criticism of past studies, see Kenneth Kressel, Labor Mediation: An Exploratory Survey ([Albany, N.Y.]: ALMA, 1972), p. 29; Charles M. Rehmus, "The Mediation of Industrial Conflict: A Note on the Literature," Journal of Conflict Resolution, 9 (March 1965): 118 and 124; Simkin in SPIDR, 1973, p. 16; Michael E. Gordon and Aaron J. Nurick, "Psychological Approaches to the Study of Unions and Union-Management Relations," Psychological Bulletin, 90 (Sept. 1981): 295, 300.

10. Newman in PERS, pp. 197-98; Tener, p. 67; Fisher and Ury, ch. 4 and 118-22; Thomas Colosi,

"Negotiation and Dispute Resolution: A Process Perspective," SPIDR, 1982, p. 71. Nonetheless, Kochan notes that pressure tactics are less effective with experienced negotiators, p. 281.

11. Most writers on mediation stress this point; see Zack, p. 82; Colosi, p. 72.

12. See Zack, pp. 61-62 and 73, 97. Kolb bases her distinction between the two types of practitioners on how the federal and state mediators whom she observed used this tactic.

13. Tener in SPIDR, 1982, p. 66.

14. Discussed by Weinberg in "Bureaucratic," pp. 11-15, and "Ethics," pp. 14-16.

15. Possibly their tendency to enter disputes earlier was related to their greater emphasis on technical assistance, a concern that was not covered by the survey.

CHAPTER 8. INTERPRETING OBSERVED DIFFERENCES:
THE JOB AND THE SYSTEM

Introduction

In the preceding chapters we discussed the differences between 1985 mediators when considered by agency affiliation and by types of cases normally handled, and we described how their demographic characteristics and attitudes changed between the 1960s and 1985. These comparisons were based on calculations of percentage differences.

Now we will investigate the extent to which further statistical analysis helps to explain the previously noted differences. Do the results substantiate the earlier, tentative conclusion that whether or not mediators found satisfaction in their client relationships explained their degree of job satisfaction? It should be noted that the purpose of this chapter is not so much to describe mediator attitudes, which were the subject of chapters 4 through 7, but rather to see what overall patterns, if any, their responses to the 1985 questionnaire followed.

The 1960s Rutgers study revealed important differences between state and federal mediators. Subsequently it was argued that the observed differences could be explained by the concentration of state agencies on public sector disputes. In this discussion, therefore, we will analyze the divergence between state and FMCS mediators, on the one hand, and between mediators who usually handle public sector and private sector cases in terms of demographic characteristics and job satisfaction. Our goal is to determine how much of the previously observed differences can be explained by education, age, length of service as a mediator and prior work history.

Job Satisfaction

One notable difference between mediators employed by state agencies and those who worked for the FMCS was the degree of satisfaction that they received from their work. A series of demographic characteristics and job attributes were tested to see whether the difference persisted when the

100

responses were subdivided according to them (or, in more technical terminology, they where used as control variables). Job satisfaction proved to be a very complex phenomenon, and the control variables interacted with each other.

The variables which appeared to be significantly related to job satisfaction were client relationships, salary satisfaction, agency affiliation, age and type of cases normally handled, in that order. Whether or not mediators reported that they were happy with their work was not significantly related to length of service, education and amount of variety that they experienced on their job, although these factors helped explain why federal mediators expressed greater satisfaction than did their state colleagues.

In chapter 4 we noted that state mediators reported significantly less satisfaction with their work than FMCS staff and that mediators who usually handled public sector cases were also less satisfied than their colleagues who handled private sector disputes. In both cases there was more than thirty percentage points difference between the attitudes of the two groups being compared, although the difference was greater when the responses were tabulated by agency rather than by type of cases handled (35.4% and 31.4%, respectively; both relationships were significant at the <.02 level).

When the responses were analyzed according to agency tenure, mediators who worked for the same agency for ten to eighteen years reacted to the question of whether they were satisfied in virtually the same proportion regardless of whether they were employed by a state agency or by the FMCS and whether they normally handled public or private sector cases. These mediators were more likely to express "very much" satisfaction than was the statistically average mediator. Thus the difference between the two groups is "explained" in that more mediators with ten to eighteen years of experience worked for the federal than for the state agencies and they handled more private than public sector disputes.

The category, very satisfied with client relationships, removed all difference between state

and federal respondents and between mediators who
handled private and public sector cases (Table
1). We therefore hypothesize that the lower
level of job satisfaction expressed by state and
public sector mediators was linked to the smaller
degree of satisfaction that they found in their
client relationships.

TABLE 1. Job Satisfaction, by Agency:
Controlling for Mediation Experience
and for Satisfactory Client Relationships
(in percentages)

Level of job satisfaction	10-18 years experience		very satisfactory client relations	
	FMCS	state	FMCS	state
mild	31.6	30.4	13.7	13.7
high	68.4	69.6	86.3	86.3
percent difference	2.4		.0	
significance	1.00		1.00	

Job Satisfaction,
by Type of Cases Normally Handled:
Controlling for Mediation Experience
and for Satisfactory Client Relationships
(in percentages)

Level of job satisfaction	10-18 years experience		very satisfactory client relations	
	private sector	public sector	private sector	public sector
mild	28.6	29.6	12.4	18.8
high	71.4	70.4	87.6	87.2
percent difference	2.0		.8	
significance	1.00		1.00	

Several other factors which, theoretically,
might have influenced the mediators' job satisfaction appear in reality to have had very little

impact. Only education and salary satisfaction seemed to play a role, albeit a minor one (they reduced the percentage difference between public and private sector mediators to 7.2% and 4.6%, respectively).

Both education and salary satisfaction were linked with age. As seen in Figure 1, education was inversely related to age. The profile of mediators in Chapter 3 showed that state mediators tended to be younger than FMCS staff members. Thus salary differences were related to age for two reasons; not only were younger mediators less senior, but they also worked for the lower paying state agencies. We consequently expected, and indeed found, a relationship between age and job satisfaction. One might also speculate that the younger, better educated mediators who worked for state agencies and received lower salaries would feel frustrated by their lack of economic rewards.

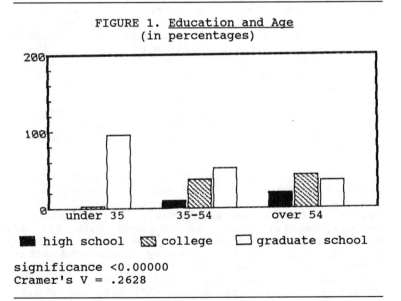

FIGURE 1. Education and Age
(in percentages)

significance <0.00000
Cramer's V = .2628

The relationship between age and job satisfaction is significant (at the <.0253 level), but it is not a strong one (Cramer's V = .1712). It is a positive relationship in that satisfaction increases with age. Thus only 48% of the mediators under 35 reported high satisfaction, whereas 70% of those between 35 and 54 and 74.5% of those over 54 said that they were very satisfied.

The difference between high and mild satisfaction appeared to be related to education. Among mediators with only a high school education, age made very little (4.4%) difference, whereas the relationship between age and job satisfaction was stronger for mediators who had attended college than for the statistically average mediator (significant at the <.0271 level and the percentage difference was 64%).

A far stronger relationship existed between job satisfaction and having satisfactory dealings with clients. Although the relationship appeared to be equally strong whether the respondents were classified by agency or types of cases (both significant at the <.00 level with phi of .2826 and .2951 respectively), some overlap existed. There was virtually no difference (2.6%) in degree of satisfaction among all mediators who handled public sector cases, regardless of agency affiliation. Presumably, therefore, federal mediators were, at least in part, happier with their client relationships and ultimately with their work because very few of them handled public sector cases. Unlike state agencies, the FMCS tended to assign public sector disputes to older, more experienced mediators and thereby avoided creating frustration among their younger staff.

Mediators who handled public sector cases more often expressed mixed feelings toward their clients (that is, 80% of those who usually handled private sector cases found their relationships to be very satisfactory, as compared with 52% of those who worked primarily in the public sector). Another factor that apparently influenced attitudes toward the parties to a dispute was level of education, although this was more true for the difference between state and FMCS than for public as opposed to private sector mediators. Thus, for example, there was only a 8.4% difference in attitude toward client relationships between state and FMCS mediators with a high school education. On the other hand, there was a 24% difference between mediators with the same level of education who handled public and private sector cases.

We can therefore attribute part of the higher satisfaction expressed by federal mediators to the larger proportion of them who had only a high school education (15.8% as compared with 7.3% of the state mediators). Interestingly enough, neither prior work experience nor length of service as a mediator explained an appreciable amount of the observed differences in satisfactory client relationships.

Two other ways of measuring attitudes toward current employment are the degree of satisfaction that an individual feels with his career and his intention of remaining in the same occupation. In the responses to the 1985 survey, career satisfaction was related both to salary satisfaction (Cramer's V = .2504) and education (V = .2921) but it was not significantly related to age, types of cases normally handled or agency affiliation.

The finding that all respondents with only a high school education were satisfied with their career while only 75% of those with a graduate education were content is consistent with the pattern of responses for job satisfaction. Both agency and types of cases handled, when used as control variables, increased rather than diminished the observed differences between the responses of mediators at various educational levels (the percentage difference for state and public sector was 48.5%, for federal it was 45% and for private sector, 37%). Thus mediators with a graduate education did not express less satisfaction with their career because more of them worked for a state agency rather than for the FMCS. It appears more accurate to conclude that advanced education by itself contributed to less rewarding client contacts.

Unlike career satisfaction, the desire to remain in mediation showed no significant relationship with educational achievement. It was, however, linked with age, agency and type of cases normally handled. Of these ties, the strongest was with age. Level of education worked in the

same direction as age, and when the two factors
were added together, the result was even more
dramatic; within the same age group, the better
educated mediators had less of a desire to remain
in the profession.

FIGURE 2. <u>Career Plans, by Age</u>
(in percentages)

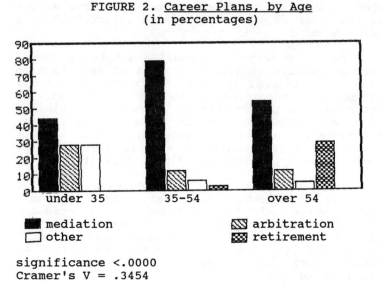

significance <.0000
Cramer's V = .3454

Elaboration of the relationship between the
several variables used to measure mediator attitudes toward their work reveals that age played a
key role. Among age groups, the same proportion
of federal and state mediators wished to remain in
the profession. Younger mediators were the least
interested in staying (since all but one of the
under-35 respondents had attended graduate school,
education was not a factor). Middle-aged mediators showed the greatest desire to remain in their
current occupation regardless of educational
level. Eighty-five percent of the mediators aged
35 to 54 with only a high school education, compared with 55% of the over-54 respondents, intended to remain in mediation. The figures for

mediators who had had some college education were 84% and 52%, and for those with some graduate education, 64% and 49%.

The declining interest in remaining in the field expressed by mediators who were 54 years or older probably reflected their desire to retire, to become arbitrators or to follow other careers. Agency affiliation, however, made a significant difference in the plans of the mediators who chose to leave the profession. Retirement was a more common choice for federal than for state mediators; more than twice the proportion of FMCS as state mediators planned to withdraw from all remunerative work (34% and 15%, respectively). State mediators who did not consider retirement as an alternative planned to become arbitrators (23% of the state mediators as compared with 6% of the FMCS respondents who were 54 years or older).

The difference in future plans between federal and state mediators who had the longest tenure with their current agencies (nineteen or more years) is even more revealing. Among them, 9% of the state mediators hoped to retire within the next five years, whereas 38% of their federal colleagues expressed that intention. Not only did 16% more of the state mediators anticipate becoming arbitrators, but there was a 13% difference between the two groups in the proportion that expected to go into another occupation (which might include retirement and part-time work). Presumably these career plans reflect differences between federal and state retirement programs.

In conclusion, we might describe the statistically average satisfied mediator as a middle-aged FMCS staff member who in 1985 had served that agency between ten and eighteen years and who handled private sector cases. He had had some graduate education, liked working with his clients, and was satisfied with his salary. However, this composite portrait is misleading in at least one respect; it masks the dissatisfaction and frustration revealed by several mediators who had attended graduate school.

Attitudes Toward Unions and Collective Bargaining
Mediators generally agreed on various issues

concerning collective bargaining and scope of bargaining, and they differed significantly on only
two of the statements designed to measure attitudes toward unions. For example, there was
little difference between the way that state and
federal mediators responded to the proposition
that collective bargaining promotes industrial
peace. There was even less difference between
mediators who handled public and private sector
disputes.

Controlling for types of cases normally
handled increased slightly (from 5.8% to 9.4%) the
difference in attitudes toward industrial relations issues between state and federal mediators
who dealt with public sector clients, but it did
not reveal a statistically significant relationship. The 24% difference between state and
federal mediators who usually handled private
sector cases was more dramatic, but it was due in
large part to the 17% of the state mediators who
either did not answer or were unsure.

Although the similarities between federal and
state responses were not quite as striking on the
other collective bargaining issues, it might
safely be concluded that the 1980s mediators
firmly believed in the industrial relations system
that developed under the NLRA. They were willing
to reduce managerial discretion when they considered broader public interests to be at stake,
and they agreed that unions had had a beneficial
influence. Neither employment history nor experience in the public, as opposed to the private,
sector appeared to exert a significant influence
on mediator opinions on these topics. Those
mediators who normally handled public sector cases
tended to agree slightly more among themselves
than did their colleagues who handled private industry disputes, but the difference was so small
that it might well have been due to chance.

Mediators differed significantly on certain
issues involving unions. State mediators and
those who normally handled public sector cases
expressed a high degree of uncertainty as to
whether unions should cooperate to help troubled
companies (24% as compared with 11% of those who
handled private sector cases) and whether unions
limited the ability of American industries to com-

pete on international markets (18% of the state
mediators were uncertain, as were 9% of the FMCS
respondents).

There was no significant difference between
mediators on the question of whether unions
prevent superior workers from advancing (two-
thirds to three-quarters of all respondents
disagreed). But, as might be expected, there was
greater disagreement between mediators who had or
had not at one time worked for a union than between any other two groups.

The relationship between types of cases normally handled and opinion as to whether unions
should help troubled companies was not a strong
one, and it was due largely to the uncertainty
expressed by mediators who usually heard public
sector disputes. Twenty-two percent of the state
mediators and 25% of the FMCS who handled public
sector cases were undecided on this question.
Even one-fourth of the former union officials who
in 1985 mediated public sector disputes were
uncertain as to whether unions should assist their
employers, while less than 10% of those who dealt
with private sector clients expressed indecision.

State and federal mediators differed significantly on the issue of whether union demands made
it difficult for American companies to compete on
the international market, although the difference
decreased when responses were classified by type
of cases handled. The relationship between
agency affiliation and attitude toward this statement was explained in part by the differing proportion of federal mediators who at one time
worked for a union. Not only were former union
employees less likely to agree with the proposition, but they were more decisive; while 18% of
all state respondents either did not respond or
were uncertain about this question, only 8% of
those who had held a paid union position were
unable to make up their minds.

Former union employment also influenced the
position that mediators took on the question of
whether unions prevent superior workers from
advancing. On the other hand, although responses
followed a similar pattern, such variables as past
experience as a manager or supervisor, agency

affiliation or type of cases normally handled did
not exert a significant influence. Figure 3 shows
that the responses of state mediators and those
who normally handled public sector cases paralleled those of mediators who had never worked for
a union. The attitudes of the FMCS staff and
those who usually handled private sector cases
were similar to those expressed by former union
employees.

FIGURE 3. <u>Unions Hinder Superior Workers,
by Agency, by Type of Cases Normally Handled
and by Past Union Employment</u>
(in percentages)

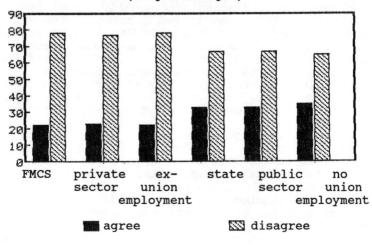

Use of more elaborate statistical analysis
demonstrates that, on the whole, the respondents
to the 1985 mediator survey supported the American
collective bargaining system, that they held positive attitudes toward unions and that they agreed
that management prerogatives might be limited in
questions that involved the interests of the sur-
rounding community.[2] Whether or not mediators
had at one time worked for a union influenced responses to propositions that implied value judgments about labor organizations.

In general the differences on collective bargaining issues revealed by the survey can be attributed to the uncertainty expressed by state mediators who normally handled public sector disputes. For them questions of whether unions should help troubled companies or whether big units made collective bargaining less effective were relatively insignificant issues to which they had devoted little thought or attention.

Attitudes Toward the Mediators' Role in Collective Bargaining

Most mediators believed that they should not permit their idea of equity to interfere with set-tlements. But they differed significantly on other issues of professional responsibility. Several of these issues divided mediators by type of cases handled rather than by agency affiliation, and their responses perhaps reflect the different needs and experiences of public sector collective bargaining.

More than 80% of the state and federal re-spondents rejected the idea that they were pri-marily responsible for representing "the public interest rather than [serving] the parties." They were almost as emphatic about the proposition that they should serve the public's main interest, "which is to maintain productivity."

Attitudes toward their role differed signifi-cantly when responses were tabulated according to type of cases normally handled (24% and 28% total difference between public and $_3$private sector mediators for the two questions).[3] Interestingly enough, mediators were somewhat more willing to accept the proposition when "public interest" was defined as maintaining productivity, and private sector mediators felt slightly more responsible toward the community at large than did those who handled public sector cases.[4]

Managerial experience did not "explain" the difference on the second question, while an analy-sis which used prior union employment revealed an 8% difference. Mediators who had only a high school education and those who had served with their agency for ten to eighteen years reacted similarly to these questions.

Thus differences between mediators who handled public and private sector cases on questions involving public responsibility cannot be attributed solely to their differing clientele. Instead, they can in part be explained by the large proportion of young former government employees or private practitioners with a college or graduate education who handled disputes in the public sector rather than in private industry.

Type of cases normally handled was not significantly related to the question of whether mediators were responsible for ensuring that settlements adhered to restrictions established by law or by executive guidelines. Although this was a more controversial issue in the early 1960s, when the federal government attempted to impose a wage freeze, it continued to arise, and it led to significant differences between state and FMCS mediators. The relationship was not strong (it had a phi of .1864). Nonetheless, the only test variable that explained a noticeable amount of the difference was graduate education, which reduced it from 27% to 11%.[5] Work history, including length of service as a mediator, had very little effect.

Summary and Conclusions

Detailed statistical analysis was used to investigate the extent to which observed relationships in attitudes toward the American collective bargaining system and the mediators' role within it could be attributed to such demographic characteristics as age, educational background and employment history. Applying the standard statistical tests for determining whether relationships existed, several were discovered, but none of them was very strong.

Job satisfaction was found to be linked to a complex of work-related characteristics which included attitude toward client relationships, degree of salary satisfaction and type of cases normally handled. According to these findings, mediators with ten to eighteen years of service, with only a high school education and who were more than 54 years old tended to be more satisfied than their colleagues. An analysis of such indirect indices of job satisfaction as career satisfaction and career plans revealed similar results.

Federal and state mediators remained firmly committed to the American collective bargaining system and, in general, believed that unions had had a beneficial impact on American life. Differences in type of cases normally handled did significantly influence these attitudes. State mediators expressed somewhat greater uncertainty on questions regarding unions, and they tended to be slightly more critical of labor organizations than their FMCS colleagues. This difference can be attributed to the higher percentage of federal mediators who at one time worked for a union.

Whether a mediator generally handled public or private sector disputes influenced attitudes toward mediator responsibility, especially when public interest was defined in terms of maintaining productivity. Differences in work history between mediators who handled public or private sector cases helped to explain divergent attitudes toward their professional responsibilities, while mediators who had attended graduate school were more likely to believe that they were responsible for seeing that settlements stayed within statutory limits.

1. For the FMCS/state cross tabulation, the level of significance was <.0020, Cramer's V = .22273 and the percentage difference was 43.5%. For public/private the figures were: level of significance, <.0382, V = .1678, percentage difference, 32.2%.

2. Questions of whether subcontracting and plant relocation should fall within the scope of bargaining and whether managements should be required to provide unions with financial data. Since mediators did not differ significantly on these items, they were not included in this discussion.

3. The relationship was not strong, however. Phi was .1641 for the more general question and .1509 for "maintaining productivity."

4. Seven percent of the public sector and 19% of the private sector mediators agreed that they should serve the public interest, generally defined while the figures were 20.5% and 35% for serving public interest in maintaining productivity.

5. Ten percent of the federal and 24% of the state mediators believed that they were responsible for adherence to laws, while 15.5% of all the mediators who had attended graduate school accepted this responsibility.

CHAPTER 9. INTERPRETING OBSERVED DIFFERENCES
ON PROFESSIONAL ISSUES AND MEDIATION TACTICS

We have analyzed the relationship between various demographic characteristics, agency affiliation, type of cases handled and responses to the 1985 survey on questions relating to job satisfaction and the American industrial relations system. In this chapter we will see whether any relationship exists between these factors and attitudes toward professional issues in mediation. We will retest our tentative conclusion that, although there were noticeable differences between mediators employed by state and federal agencies and between those who normally handled public or private sector disputes concerning matters of professional policy and tactics, these differences did not follow the consistent pattern observed in Massachusetts by Debora Kolb.

Professional Issues

In Chapter 7 we noted that in 1985 most mediators believed that the public at large did not appreciate the importance of their services, but that unions (and to a lesser extent managers) recognized their value. Significant differences existed among the respondents, however, concerning attitudes toward mediator-client relationships. The relevant questions were, Should mediators specialize? Should they handle the same clients in subsequent labor disputes? And should they follow cases if negotiations moved to a new site?

For all but the last question, mediator responses differed significantly both according to agency affiliation and to type of cases normally handled.[1] Much of the difference was explained by years of mediation experience. Prior employment history only helped to explain disagreement over whether mediators should establish permanent relationships with clients, while level of education explained some of the difference on that question as well as on the issue of whether mediators should specialize. Interestingly enough, whether or not mediators were satisfied with their general client relationships did not explain differences in mediator responses to these questions, nor did prior management experience.

Taking one question, whether mediators should keep the same clients in subsequent disputes, as an example (in Figure 1), we find that a modest majority of the FMCS respondents were favorable and that most of the difference was due to the 22% "undecided" state responses. When this factor was eliminated we find that mediators who had worked for the same agency from ten to eighteen years had similar attitudes regardless of types of cases handled or agency affiliation. No other variable eliminated as much (19%) of the difference.

FIGURE 1. <u>Mediators Should Retain Clientele, by Agency</u>
(in percentages)

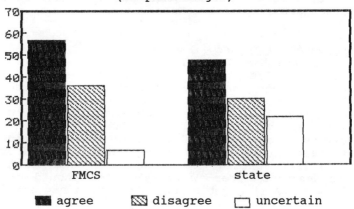

significance <.0029
Cramer's V = .2200
percentage difference 30.1

Rather unsurprisingly, responses to the question of whether mediators should retain jurisdiction if the site of negotiation changed followed the same pattern. Those with one or two decades of service as mediators were more interested in continuity than their colleagues who had either more or less experience.

Reactions to the proposition that mediators should specialize followed a slightly different pattern. Both agency affiliation and type of cases handled showed comparatively strong and significant relationships to responses. More than two-thirds of the percentage difference between mediators disappeared (that is the difference fell from 42% to 12%) when nineteen or more years agency service was used as an explanatory variable. Controlling for high school education also diminished the difference between state and FMCS mediators (from 42% to 25%). Calculation of relationships according to whether the respondents handled private or public sector disputes revealed a similar pattern.

Another topic of interest to the mediation profession is the question of whether intervention by two or more neutrals benefits either mediators or parties to the dispute. Mediators differed significantly on both of these questions, and the relationship between attitude and either agency or type of cases handled was stronger than many of the relationships discussed heretofore. Once again, undecided responses played a significant role (Figure 2, next page).

Former work experience explained more of the difference between groups of respondents regarding dual or panel mediation than did years of experience or educational level. Further analysis revealed that the high proportion of undecided responses was due to mediators who at one time or another had held a supervisory or managerial position. Thus 28.2% of the FMCS and 32.3% of the state respondents who at one time had held a management position could not decide whether dual mediation was satisfactory for the parties. But they were more certain about whether dual mediation was satisfactory for them in their capacity as mediators (the figures were still high at 13.2% for FMCS with former managerial experience and 16.1% for state staff members.)

These examples show that no one variable consistently influenced mediators' attitudes toward client relationships. Although on several important questions the attitudes of those who normally heard public sector disputes differed from those expressed by private sector mediators, the varia-

FIGURE 2. <u>Dual Mediation Satisfies Parties</u>,
<u>by Agency</u>
(in percentages)

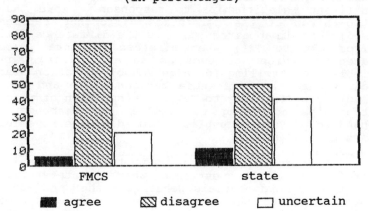

significance <.0004
Cramer's V = .2551
percentage difference 50.0

<u>Dual Mediation Unsatisfactory</u>
<u>for Mediators, by Agency</u>
(in percentages)

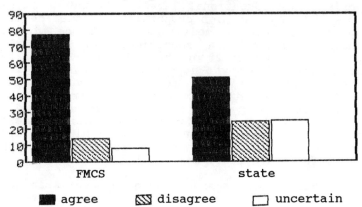

significance <.0000
Cramer's V = .2867
percentage difference 52.8

tions were not explained by the differences in educational level, length of service and prior work experience that characterized the two groups.

Voluntarism and Dependence

Participants in the survey were asked several questions which measured their attitudes toward the voluntary nature of the American collective bargaining system and the extent to which they believed themselves to be bound by their clients' wishes. Mediators agreed that, in general, they should not enter disputes without the consent of the parties and that they should withdraw if they became unwelcome to either side. Nonetheless, there was a significant difference in the reaction of state and federal mediators, as well as of those who normally handled public or private sector cases, to the statement that, with rare exceptions, they should not enter without the parties' consent.

Significant differences (16%) existed in the attitudes of mediators who handled public and private sector cases on the question of not entering uninvited. These differences were related to the length of time that the respondent had worked for the same agency (those with nineteen or more years had virtually the same opinion regardless of type of cases handled) and to college education (the difference between public and private sector mediators fell to 6%). Moreover, none of the mediators with the most experience and/or with a college education were undecided. On the other hand, the relationship between agency affiliation and responses to the question of entering without an invitation was not as strong (Cramer's V = .1983 as compared with .2037), and educational level did not explain the observed differences.

The mediators' reactions to questions concerning compulsory arbitration were interesting, if not entirely consistent. Participants in the survey were asked whether labor-management negotiations should be subject to compulsory arbitration generally, or in the case of public sector disagreements, or only where health care facilities were involved. The questions were phrased identically so that semantic differences would not affect responses.

It might be predicted that mediator responses to questions concerning specific types of cases would demonstrate greater differences than would replies to the general proposition that all collective bargaining disputes should be subject to compulsory arbitration. This was true to a degree. Although reactions to the general proposition differed significantly by agency and by types of cases handled, the various groups reacted similarly to the proposition that all intractable public sector disputes should be submitted to compulsory arbitration (approximately 30% favored, 60% opposed and 10% were undecided as to whether this was a wise policy). Such explanatory factors as prior employment history, length of service as a mediator or educational background did not exert a significant influence.

Mediators disagreed most strongly about the suggestion that health care cases should be subject to compulsory arbitration (18.2% difference on the general question compared with 52.4% on health care disputes). Attitudes toward this question evidently were influenced by the respondents' educational achievements and by prior employment. The less well educated mediators with prior experience in industrial relations opposed compulsory arbitration for health care disputes more strongly than did their colleagues who had attended college or graduate school and had worked either for a government agency or who had independent professional practices (40% of all state mediators opposed, as did 62.5% of the state mediators with a high school education and 52.6% of those who had once been employed by a union).[2]

If, perhaps, the question regarding public sector disputes had distinguished between fire and police disputes on the one hand and negotiations with clerical or school employees on the other, mediator responses to that question would have paralleled their answers to the health care question.[3] Since the distinction was not made we, are unable to generalize further about the impact of education and industrial relations experience on mediator attitudes toward compulsory arbitration when issues of public health and safety were at stake.

Mediators reacted consistently to a series of questions about their dependence on the parties to the dispute; agency affiliation, type of cases handled, and length of mediation experience seemed to have little influence on how they responded to the issue of whether, when meeting separately with one side, they were permitted to support vigorously a position taken by the other party, or whether, when conveying a proposal to the other side, they were required to reflect accurately the degree of pressure that the original party would exert.

They only question on which there was significant (16.8%) difference was: "The best way to exploit pressure in negotiations is to have the parties exert it face-to-face." The relationship was strengthened when only the mediators who handled private sector cases were considered; the percentage of difference rose to 46.8%. The determining factor was the high proportion (25%) of state mediators who were undecided on this issue. This is another example of the point made earlier that state mediators tended to be less decided about professional issues and that their experience in government agencies or private professional practices did not provide them with ready opinions concerning mediation issues.[4]

Tactics and Strategy

The participants in the 1985 survey agreed on most tactics although they differed significantly, both by agency and by type of cases handled, on questions of timing and on selecting the single best tactic for settling a dispute. Further analysis revealed some interesting differences which shed light on Kolb's characterization of state mediators as more active interventionists and of FMCS staff as facilitators.[5]

Responses to the question of whether it is better for mediators to be forceful than to be timid are relevant to this distinction. Most mediators agreed to the proposition. In fact, the only group that differed significantly, mediators with more than eighteen years experience, did not follow the predicted pattern. Contrary to what Kolb predicted, 97% of the federal mediators and only 67% of the state mediators who had served for

nineteen or more years agreed that forcefulness
was better than timidity.[6]

Although the relationship does not meet the
criteria for statistical reliability used in this
study, the figures for mediators who had served
between ten and eighteen years provide an interesting contrast in that the proportions of mediators who handled public and private sector cases
and who favored forcefulness was reversed. Almost
all state mediators with this length of service
who handled public sector cases believed a
forceful personality to be better. For their
part, there was some difference of opinion among
FMCS staff and those who handled private sector
cases. In the ten to eighteen year service
category, the proportion of "undecided" responses
was low. On the other hand, 25% of the state
mediators (and 20% of those who handled public
sector cases) with nineteen or more years of
service in the same agency,were undecided.

Thus length of service apparently exerted
more influence over whether a mediator valued
forcefulness above timidity than did agency affiliation or type of cases handled. One-fifth
more of the state mediators and those who handled
public sector disputes with ten to eighteen years
of service than the average mediator regarded
forcefulness as desirable while, among mediators
with eighteen or more years service, approximately
one-third more of the FMCS staff and those who
handled private sector cases than the average
mediator agreed with the proposition.

Another issue which allegedly reflects philo-
sophic differences concerning the degree to which
mediators should intervene in the bargaining process is the question of when mediators should
enter disputes. This problem had long separated
state and FMCS mediators, and their differing responses reflected attitudes toward such practices
as preventive mediation which were common in the
federal system but not in state agencies.

Participants in the survey were asked two
separate questions: When, theoretically, is the
best time to enter a dispute, and at what stage
during the previous year had the respondent
actually become involved? There were significant

differences in answers to both of the questions, whether analyzed by[7] agency affiliation or by type of cases handled. The relationship between theoretical timing and agency, as well as with type of cases, was comparatively strong and was not explained by any of the test variables. In fact, such explanatory variables as prior employment and type of cases increased, rather than reduced, the difference and strengthened the relationship. Using one variable as an example, "no management background," we find that the percentage difference increased from 75% to 89%, but the pattern of responses remained the same (Table 1). This example supports the conclusion that federal and state mediators continued to disagree significantly about the proper time to intervene.[8]

TABLE 1. When Enter, in Theory, by Agency: Controlling for No Management Experience
(in percentages)

When enter	FMCS	state	controlling for no management experience FMCS	state
well underway	62.1	24.7	65.0	20.6
at impasse	37.9	75.3	35.0	79.4
significance	< .00		.00	
phi		.3670		.4313
percentage difference		74.8		88.8

Responses to the question of when mediators actually entered disputes during the previous year followed the same pattern; they differed significantly by agency and type of cases handled, but, with the exception of "enter at the beginning," these differences were more strongly related to agency affiliation than to differences in type of cases.

Entering at the beginning implies a paternalistic attitude -- possibly even a modified form of preventive mediation -- while waiting until the parties have reached an impasse provides them with the greatest opportunity to achieve their own settlement. It must be remembered, however, that deadlines have less practical meaning in the public sector, at least in jurisdictions where strikes by government employees are forbidden by law. Hence there is less reason for mediators to intervene early in most public sector negotiations.

The responses to the questionnaire support these generalizations; 69% of the state and 55% of the FMCS mediators reported that in 1984 they had entered no disputes at the beginning of negotiations. Among mediators who usually handled public sector cases, the figure was 74%, and it was 51% for those who usually handled private sector cases (the percentage difference was 28% when calculated by agency and 46% by type of cases).

Looking at the effect of several test variables, the only one that helped explain the difference between mediators on the proportion of cases that they entered early in negotiations was prior employment. Paid union employment explained a sizeable amount of the difference among mediators whether classified by agency affiliation or type of cases normally handled (this relationship was not significant, however).

Finally, the only variable that explained the difference between FMCS and state mediators as to the proportion of cases entered when the dispute was well underway was type of cases normally handled. High school education reduced the difference from 43% to 7.6% when mediators were classified by type of cases normally handled.

Data concerning when mediators entered cases leads to the tentative conclusion that one-time union employment encouraged some state and public sector mediators to intervene earlier in practice (58% of the state mediators who had once worked for a union entered no cases at the beginning, compared to 69% of all state mediators; the figures for those who handled public sector cases were 67% and 74%). The relationship does not, however, hold true for FMCS mediators.

That mediators who handled public sector cases were less prone than those who handled private sector disputes to enter at an early stage was confirmed by using type of cases as a control variable. No other variable either explained an appreciable amount of the difference or showed a particularly strong relationship. It is not surprising, therefore, that no other control variable reduced the difference between mediators, when classified by type of cases handled, on the question of when, in practice, they entered disputes (the relationship was significant at the $<.0008$ level, with phi = .2295).

In conclusion, it is clear that differences in timing, which predated the growth of public sector collective bargaining, continued through 1985 and were reinforced by increasing differentiation between state and FMCS mediators as to whether they normally mediated private or public sector disputes. Except for early entry, however, the relationship with agency affiliation remained stronger than with type of cases handled. Past employment experience and length of service as a mediator helped to explain some of the observed differences, but they did not exert an across-the-board influence and certainly did not explain why state mediators tended to enter later than did federal mediators.

Instead, differences between mediators who generally handled public and private sector disputes may well be attributed to institutional and legal differences. The most important of these differences are the various laws which forbid strikes in public employment and make fact-finding and/or interest arbitration the final steps in the dispute settlement system. Since strike deadlines do not exist, there is less pressure to settle, and mediators in public sector disputes enter at later stages in negotiations than their colleagues whose clients may resort to strikes or lockouts. Unfortunately, it was impossible to use the existence or non-existence of no-strike laws within the mediator's jurisdiction as a test variable, and the affect of this factor remains speculative.

On the other hand, the FMCS had long been interested in providing technical assistance to the parties and viewed its mission, at least in part, as an educational one. Hence its mediators were, perhaps, disposed to enter disputes earlier in order to train their clients in dispute resolution techniques.[9]

Mediators showed a remarkable degree of unity when asked to rank in order of effectiveness a series of tactics designed to encourage settlement. They agreed most strongly on which tacatics were the least desirable but showed less uniformity in labeling techniques as helpful (Chapter 7, Table 2). Thus they agreed that appeals to rank, status or implied force were inappropriate.

Differences regarding the two techniques which proved to be the most controversial, emphasizing the mediators' status as public representatives and appealing to the desirability of settling through mutual consent, were explained in part by length of experience and level of education. State mediators with less experience but with some graduate education rated the use of their status as representatives of the public interest higher than did their FMCS colleagues and those with longer mediation experience and less education. On the other hand, college educated mediators placed more faith in developing an atmosphere of mutual consent than did mediators with less than nine years of experience, who also were more likely to have attended graduate school.[10]

Nowhere does this analysis indicate that state and FMCS staff or mediators who handled either public and private sector cases used significantly different techniques for settling disputes. Still, their experience led them to emphasize more strongly one or another way of manipulating status. Thus 55% of the state mediators ranked use of status as a representative of the public higher than next to least effective; 34.5% of the FMCS staff agreed with this rating. Mediators who handled public sector disputes ranked an appeal to the benefit of mutual consent lower than did their colleagues who handled private sector cases. Still, the differences were too small to establish a different ranking scale for state and

FMCS mediators or for those who handled public or private sector cases.

Other techniques were discussed earlier in the sections that examined the degree to which mediators believed themselves to be bound by the parties' wishes and their attitudes toward the voluntary nature of the American collective bargaining system. Mediators overwhelmingly agreed that they should deflate extreme positions and that a forceful mediator was better than a timid one. Nonetheless, they strongly believed that "bossy" tactics were least likely to achieve a settlement. They disapproved of publishing recommendations in an effort to exert pressure on the parties and were evenly divided as to whether they should play the devil's advocate when discussing positions in separate sessions.

Summary and Conclusions
Mediators viewed themselves as generalists, rejecting both the idea of specializing or of establishing their own clientele. Sentiment for creating a continuing relationship with parties was strong only among mediators with ten to eighteen years experience (but only 60% of them expressed the desire). Attitudes toward dual mediation[11] revealed a dislike of external intervention which was stronger among federal than state mediators. State mediators were reluctant to judge whether dual mediation served the interests of the parties, however.

Mediators, on the whole, respected the parties' right to decide if they wanted mediation, but they disagreed as to whether arbitration should be the final step for all or for some types of disputes. Interestingly enough, the greatest disagreement arose over health care cases; state mediators were more likely to favor compulsory arbitration even though FMCS mediators handled more of the disputes in that industry. Education and union experience partly explained the differences among mediators on this issue.

Analysis of attitudes toward mediation techniques and strategies did not reveal a clear-cut pattern of differences between state and federal

staff or between mediators who handled public and
private sector cases which would permit their description as more or less active interveners in the
collective bargaining process. In fact, statistically significant differences between mediators
often can be attributed to the larger proportion
of mediators employed by state agencies and those
who handled public sector disputes who were uncertain or undecided as to tactics. These differences in opinion can, in turn, frequently be
traced to the higher percentage of state mediators
assigned to public sector cases who came to mediation from government agencies, from private professional practices or directly from graduate
school. Hence they lacked practical negotiating
experience.

Federal and state mediators (and to a lesser
extent mediators who handled public and private
sector cases) differed significantly as to when
they entered disputes. None of the test variables
explained an appreciable amount of the difference,
although controlling for type of cases handled did
reveal a tendency for mediators to enter public
sector cases later than private sector disputes.

When asked to evaluate techniques, all mediators placed the more coercive alternatives at the
bottom of the list. They disagreed, however, as
to whether it was better to appeal to mutual consent than to the hope for mutual benefit.   In
general, mediators did not believe appeals to
status and rank to be effective. But less experienced and more highly educated state mediators
placed greater reliance on the use of their rank
as public representatives than did their FMCS colleagues with longer mediation experience.

On the whole we might say that these differences in timing and use of rank do not reflect a
general policy of activism or passivity which
governed the mediators' choice of techniques and
strategies. Instead, responses to the 1985 survey
revealed a remarkable amount of agreement among
practitioners on many technical questions.

The explanation for this consensus may
perhaps be found in factors which could not be
measured by this particular questionnaire, given
the limits that the researchers set for themselves

-- to replicate as much as possible the study of mediator background, self-image and attitudes conducted in the early 1960s.   Hence it was not possible to investigate what kind of people were attracted to mediation[12] and what kind of candidates the FMCS and state agencies selected.   This survey nonetheless revealed that the 1980s mediators shared several characteristics and that this common core persisted despite growing differences in education and prior work experience between state and federal mediators and between those who normally handled public and private sector disputes.

NOTES

1. There was a statistically significant (at the <.000 level) difference between state and federal mediators on the question of whether mediators should specialize. But this was due to the large percentage (17%) of state mediators who were undecided. More state than federal mediators (12% as opposed to 5%) favored specialization.

2. These factors had less influence on FMCS responses, however.

3. See Chapter 6.

4. Unfortunately it was impossible to investigate whether there was a significant relationship between "undecided" responses and prior work experience and length of service as a mediator.

5. Repeated by Zack in his Public Sector Mediation as well. Both attribute this difference to the concentration of many state agencies on public sector cases.

6. When calculated either by agency or type of cases handled, the difference is too small for reliability, but both calculations fail to support Kolb's hypothesis--agreement was stronger among FMCS/private sector mediators.

7. See Table 1, Chapter 7. For 1985 the relationship was significant at <.00 with phi = .3670.

8. Only two respondents selected "enter early," and none thought that entering "at the beginning" was desirable, although several reported doing so in a small number of cases.

9. Several FMCS respondents commented on the lack of questions concerning technical assistance. They expressed mixed feelings about this program.

10. Experience and education only reduced the difference concerning "use of status" from 41% to 33% and 30%, respectively, whereas they reduced

disagreement about "use of mutual consent" from 30% to 10% and 3%.

11. As discussed elsewhere, FMCS staff did not react as strongly to participation by agency officials as the critical comments of a few respondents led one to expect. There was no comparable question on the state questionnaire, hence the issue could not be further analyzed.

12. Unfortunately, coding difficulties prevented using responses to the series of questions concerning tolerance of stress and willingness to accept risk as explanatory variables.

CHAPTER 10.   CONCLUSIONS

The preceding chapters report the findings of a 1985 survey of professional labor mediators, the men and women who were employed full-time and classified as mediators by the FMCS and by the various state labor relations agencies that belong to ALRA.   The responses were subjected to a two-fold analysis.

The first goal was to replicate an early 1960s survey of mediators which investigated their demographic characteristics, self-image and attitudes.   The results of the two studies were compared in order to determine what changes had occurred during the quarter-century interval.   New computer facilities permitted the identification of environmental conditions (both within and outside the agency) and/or demographic characteristics that helped to explain the observed differences among 1985 mediator responses.   Unfortunately, the raw data from the 1960s study was unavailable, and a similar in-depth analysis could not be undertaken for the earlier results.

Comparing the results of the two surveys revealed a number of interesting trends.   The 1985 mediators possessed significantly different demographic characteristics.   Compared with the 1960s respondents, the 1985 FMCS participants were older, while the state mediators were younger and had had less day-to-day labor relations and mediation experience.   In comparison with their FMCS colleagues, a smaller proportion of the state mediators lived with their spouses, and they came from a slightly higher social level.   As might be expected, there was little appreciable difference among FMCS regions,[1] although the Eastern mediators were older and had worked longer for the Service.   Hence they enjoyed higher family income and salaries.

The differences between state and federal mediators in educational level and work experience increased between the 1960s and 1985.   Nonetheless, the most important difference among the latter respondents was not demographic.   Instead, the discrepancy in duties and type of cases that they normally handled created what, at least on first impression, appeared to be an ever-widening gap between mediators employed by the several state agencies and by the federal service that already had been noted by Berkowitz, et. al. in their 1966 report.

Generally, state agencies combined administrative and labor board activities, while only 10% of the FMCS staff reported that they devoted an appreciable amount of time to tasks other than mediation. Furthermore, over three-quarters of the state mediators reported that more than half of their cases involved public sector disputes. While it was impractical to use the extent to which respondents performed nonmediation functions as a variable, the distinction between those who normally handled public as compared with private sector cases proved to be an useful one. Interestingly enough, however, there was only one demographic characteristic in which the difference between these two groups was greater than between state and FMCS mediators, and that was type of prior work experience.

Whether mediators usually handled public or private sector cases became a new variable for analyzing differences in opinions on various professional issues. In recent years the question has been raised in the literature as to whether the increased concentration of state staff members on public sector cases has not enlarged the difference between FMCS and state mediators' attitudes toward their work. If this assumption is true then not only should their disagreements have become greater, but the ideas of state mediators should have changed more since 1962 than those held by FMCS staff members.

Responses to the 1985 survey showed no such clear-cut pattern. Federal and state mediators alike expressed less satisfaction with their work than did their counterparts twenty-five years before, and they were less eager to remain in the profession. But the decline was greater among state than among federal mediators. On the other hand, the 1985 mediators viewed their careers more favorably than did their 1960s counterparts, and they were more likely to attribute this success to

their education. Surprisingly enough, in view of
their salary differences and their less satisfactory client relationships, state mediators rated
their career progress more highly than did the
FMCS respondents.

The intention of remaining in mediation was
linked with age, education, salary satisfaction
and good client relations.   Federal and state
mediators, as well as 1960s and 1985 mediators,
differed significantly on all of these qualities.
Thus younger, better educated mediators who reported less satisfaction with wages and client
relations also reported lower job satisfaction.
This profile describes the state as opposed to the
FMCS mediator, and, with the exception of age, it
also describes the respondents to the 1985 survey
in comparison with the 1960s participants. On the
other hand, while the 1985 state mediators found
their jobs more stressful than did their federal
colleagues, the difference between the two was
larger in the 1960s than in 1985.

The federal form included three questions
relating specifically to FMCS practices.   These
items measured attitudes toward the national office and the regional directors.   In general respondents from the Central Region expressed the
least appreciation for national office assistance
and were less likely to grant their director an
active role in mediation. But Southern FMCS staff
made the largest percentage of the remarks on
government policy, most of which were critical.
Surprisingly, however, they most consistently
expressed satisfaction with their career.[2]

In Chapters 8 and 9 detailed statistical
analysis was used to see what factors, if any,
explained the difference in mediator enthusiasm as
well as its decline since the 1960s. This analysis revealed a relationship between the desire to
remain in mediation and age; younger mediators
expressed a greater intention of leaving than
their middle-aged or older colleagues.   Apparently, state mediators found their agency retirement programs to be less attractive than did FMCS
staff, and they were less likely to anticipate
withdrawing from the labor force after twenty-five
years service than were their FMCS colleagues.[3]

Further analysis revealed that length of service and client relationships helped to explain
job satisfaction. For example, mediators who had
worked for an agency for ten to eighteen years
tended to be more satisfied regardless of agency
affiliation or type of cases handled. Degree of
satisfaction with client relationships explained
even more of the difference in job satisfaction,
and it, in turn, was related both to educational
level and type of cases normally handled.

Rather than attribute the lower job satisfaction reported by mediators who usually handled
public sector cases (and most likely worked for
state agencies) to the frustration of government
employment relations alone, differences in the
mediators' agency experience, educational level
and satisfaction with client relationships must
be considered. Of these, only client relations
was connected with conditions created by public
sector collective bargaining; the others were
related to the varying hiring policies of state
agencies as compared with the FMCS.

An analysis of mediator opinions concerning
the industrial relations system in which they
functioned and their role in it reveals that, in
1985, respondents generally expressed even more
favorable attitudes toward unions than did their
predecessors of the 1960s. Within the FMCS, the
Western staff exhibited more pro-union sympathies.
Although the responses of FMCS and state mediators
became more similar over time, the difference
between them was still larger than between mediators who usually handled private or public sector
cases.

Differences in employment background influenced mediators' opinions on economic issues
and the American industrial relations system.
FMCS mediators were more concerned about productivity and expressed greater support for the industrial relations system that developed under the
NLRA than did their state colleagues. For their
part, in 1985 fewer state mediators believed that
collective bargaining and mediation helped maintain industrial peace than did their predecessors,
and the difference between their attitudes and
those held by FMCS staff increased over the years.

The FMCS responses were classified by region in order to determine whether local economic conditions exerted an influence on attitudes toward economic questions.[4] Their reactions to several scope of bargaining questions did reflect varying regional conditions. For example, job security was more of an issue for mediators in the Central district, while the Eastern FMCS staff were more concerned about plant relocation.

Although state mediators were more likely than FMCS respondents to impose some restrictions on the parties' right to self determination, both groups were willing to limit managerial prerogatives by increasing the scope of bargaining. In the matter of whether they should intervene in negotiations without the consent of both parties, Federal and state mediators agreed more strongly in 1985 than they had in the 1960s that the parties' wishes should be respected. Responses to this question indicated that increasing concentration on public sector cases did not reduce the state mediators' respect for the voluntary nature of collective bargaining, although they thought that disputes involving public health and safety required special regulations.

Only a bare majority of FMCS and a few more state mediators favored the enactment of laws requiring recourse to mediation before either party engaged in a job action (that is, a strike or lock-out). They roundly rejected the idea of imposing compulsory arbitration on all types of industrial disputes, although the difference between federal and state mediators on this issue increased slightly between the 1960s and 1985. The difference was further increased when responses were classified according to type of cases normally handled rather than by agency affiliation.

State mediators and those who handled public sector cases experienced considerable difficulty in answering a number of questions concerning professional issues. This may well reflect their relative inexperience in industrial relations as compared with FMCS staff. For example, they were less certain about whether a mediator should follow a case if the site changed and whether the same mediator should assist if parties needed help in resolving subsequent labor disputes. Other questions on which a high percentage of state mediators were undecided concerned ad hoc and dual mediation and the virtues of specialization.

The more detailed analysis in Chapters 8 and 9 clarifies the role played by undecided responses and identifies the source of this uncertainty. Prior employment history and level of education were important factors. For example, younger and better educated mediators were less certain about dual mediation than were their colleagues with longer experience and less education. The high percentage of uncertain responses thus was also explained, in part, by the number of state mediators who at one time had held a supervisory or managerial position.

State mediators expressed more uncertainty on questions of strategy and tactics than did their federal colleagues. Even so, by 1985 the attitudes of mediators on several important questions had became more similar than they had been in the 1960s. Where it was possible to measure the difference (that is, where the question was included in the 1960s form and the responses were reported in the 1966 study), mediators in the 1980s were less likely to admit to manipulating or pressuring their clients. Still, more of them agreed with the statement that it was better to be forceful than to be timid.[5]

An increasing difference between state and FMCS mediators as to when they preferred to enter disputes probably was due more to institutional and legal differences under both state legislation and the NLRA than to differences in agency policy. Nonetheless, in the 1980s federal mediators entered disputes earlier than they had in 1964. Within the FMCS, Southern mediators preferred to enter earlier and Central staff members opted for later entry, thus indicating that this trend within the FMCS might reflect conditions in areas where collective bargaining was comparatively new.

Finally, there was greater agreement among FMCS staff than among state mediators as to how they ranked a series of settlement tactics.[6]

Mediators who handled public sector disputes
ranked an appeal to the benefits of mutual consent
higher than did their colleagues who handled
private sector cases; possibly, the pressure of
public opinion played a role.

Further study of several key questions concerning the American industrial relations system
showed that employment history, experience in the
public sector and regional economic environment
failed to exert a significant influence on mediator opinions concerning collective bargaining
issues. But employment background (specifically,
employment by a union) did affect responses to
statements that implied value judgments regarding
employee organizations. On only one question,
whether unions should help troubled companies, did
clientele apparently exert a stronger influence on
attitudes than former union employment.

Whether mediators handled public or private
sector cases influenced their attitudes toward
such questions involving professional responsibility as whether mediators primarily served the public or the parties' interest. Mediators who
handled private sector cases felt slightly more
responsible toward the community at large if
"public interest" was defined as maintaining
productivity. But this latter difference was
explained by educational level and length of
service and could not be attributed solely to the
environment created by public sector collective
bargaining.

Differences between mediators on professional
and technical issues eluded simple interpretation.
For most questions, the discrepancy between responses was greater if they were analyzed by
agency affiliation than by type of cases normally
handled. No one variable consistently influenced
mediators' opinions, and the several characteristics that distinguished FMCS and state or public
and private sector mediators did not exert a uniform effect.

In general, it can be said that mediator
attitudes tended to converge over the years between the early 1960s and 1985, although there was
no large-scale transformation. Therefore, the

seemingly dramatic environmental and psychological
changes which occurred during that quarter century, instead of intensifying the differences between mediators, appear to have increased their
similarities. A comparison of responses from the
FMCS districts confirms the more general findings
in that their attitudes rarely reflected regional
environmental differences.

In the long run, the environment of the specific agency for which the mediator worked, rather
than local factors, educational differences or
type of disputes normally handled, molded his attitudes toward professional issues. This
conclusion was reinforced by the observation that
the larger amount of uncertainty expressed by
state mediators was linked with their
comparatively shorter service within their agency
rather than their lack of preparation or
sophistication.

Thus, even if mediators' backgrounds differed
between the FMCS and state agencies, over the
years between the 1960s and 1985 agency mediation
became an increasingly professional occupation
where newcomers served their apprenticeship before
they became fully socialized into the occupational
point of view and felt qualified to express
opinions on questions of common concern. The
longer they were exposed to agency service, the
more similar their reactions became to those
expressed by colleagues employed by other
agencies.

1. Altogether, there was a statistically significant relationship for only one-fifth, or twenty,
of the 100 variables that were used to test
regional differences.

2. Westerners expressed the least satisfaction,
but this relationship was not statistically significant.

3. There is insufficient evidence to test the
hypothesis that state mediators were less likely
to have vested pension benefits from prior employment than were FMCS staff. Within the FMCS, the
largest group that anticipated retirement within
five years was in the Eastern Region.

4. It was impossible to ascertain regional differences among state mediators because, although
their responses could be coded according to state,
ALMA has an insufficient number of members in the
South to permit comparison.

5. The relevant questions were not included in the
1962 state form; hence, although one can see a
decline in FMCS approval of forceful measures, as
predicted by the Kolb theory, it was impossible to
discover whether state mediators became more mani-
pulative. But a far higher percentage of FMCS
than state mediators with eighteen or more years
of mediation experience thought that forcefulness
was better. Evidently, differences on this question were related to generational differences as
well as to agency and type of client.

6. There was virtually no difference among the
regions.

APPENDIX A: A NOTE ON METHODS

The methods employed in this study were limited by the nature of the data -- self-reported demographic and attitudinal information concerning men and women employed full time as labor mediators by either the FMCS or by the state labor relations agencies belonging to ALRA -- the number of cases (256), and the questions that were asked. Roughly parallel data from the 1960s was available in tabular form, but it was impossible to reconstruct the data sets for each respondent, and only limited use could be made of this material.

Although the methods might appear elementary to a professional statistician, they became progressively more complex as narrower questions were asked of the data. The first goal was to determine what subgroups existed within the "universe" of 1985 mediators. Starting with the given categories of FMCS and state agency staff, we asked whether the two were indeed separate entities within the larger universe -- that is, did the members of each group have more in common with each other than they had with the members of the other group?

We employed descriptive statistics to answer this question. They enabled us to draw a profile of the "average" mediator using frequency distributions for each of the demographic characteristics. On this basis state and FMCS mediators were compared with each other as well as with their counterparts studied in the early 1960s.

Simple descriptive statistics, however, do not tell whether the differences observed between two groups are real distinctions or are due to chance. Mathematicians, therefore, use the concept of probability to infer, or guess, what the likelihood is that the groups actually differed from each other. Once their independence was verified, we tried to determine whether the similarities within the groups had grown stronger or weaker over the years.

We were even more interested in discovering whether other ways of dividing our data were more accurate -- that is whether our mediators had more in common if they are classified according to agency affiliation, type of cases normally handled, prior employment, education or other demographic characteristics. Again, frequency distributions provided us with preliminary answers.

Most importantly, however, we were interested in seeing the extent to which these groups had homogeneous attitudes about themselves, the system in which they functioned and the work that they performed. This required more than tabulating responses. Because we had little choice in the questions that were asked, we could only organize the questions around abstract or complex concepts. Then we used cross tabulations to see what relationships existed between the component parts of each abstract or complex idea.

Let us take job satisfaction as an example. We hypothesized that attitudes towards work were influenced by and/or reflected in reactions to a series of job related conditions which included salary, use of skills, relations with clients, evaluation of career, evaluation of treatment by the employing agency and career plans for the following five years. We therefore tabulated the relationship between strongly positive and strongly negative responses to the question of whether they were satisfied with their work to their responses to the characteristics which presumably make up the abstraction, job satisfaction. The resulting patterns are called cross tabulations, or simultaneous tabulations of the responses to two different (but hopefully related) questions.

Probability theory is used to judge the likelihood that the distribution of responses in a cross tabulation is due to chance. The smaller the probability, the greater the likelihood that the relationship is significant or meaningful rather than accidental. Conversely, as it approaches 1.0, the probability increases that the observed distribution is due to chance. This figure is called "level of significance," and in this study only levels of less than .05 (<.05)

were regarded as significant.   In the discussion
of findings, where the level was greater but the
distribution had interesting features, the "lack
of significance" was noted.

Often the relationship between the phenomena
may be significant in that there is little likelihood that it is due to chance, but it is a weak
one -- it holds true for only part of the group
that is being described.   The statistic that
measures strength of relationship for simple two
cell tables is "phi," and for larger ones it is
Cramer's V.   Both employ a scale of .00 to +1.00;
the larger the value, the stronger the relationship.   In this study almost all of the observed
relationships were weak; their phi or Cramer's V
value generally fell well below 0.50.   This is
characteristic of most social science data.

We have used one other statistic, the percentage difference or residual.   This figure shows
the total amount of variation in a relationship.
The more different the two groups are, the greater
the percentage difference.   On the other hand,
when a third variable is added to a two cell cross
tabulation in an attempt to see whether one group
or another is more strongly characterized by what
is called an "explanatory variable," we look to
see if the introduction of this qualification
reduces the difference (or residual) between our
classes.   Small percentage differences imply that
there was little disagreement among groups of
mediators on the issue or characteristic under
consideration.

Thus, for example, we tested to see whether,
if we used former union employment as an explanatory variable, we were able to reduce the difference between state and federal mediators in attitudes toward unions.   Rather unsurprisingly, we
discovered that the attitudes of mediators who
once worked for a union, regardless of agency
affiliation or type of cases handled, showed
greater similarity than did the attitudes of the
entire mediator sample. Thus we "explained" some
of the difference in attitudes toward unions between state and federal mediators by the greater
percentage of federal mediators who at one time
worked for a union.   The amount by which the dif-

ference between state and federal attitudes was reduced is the amount that this variable explains.

In the above example, the independent variable (or the given), was agency affiliation; the dependent variable (or the one that we want to explain) was attitude toward unions; and the explanatory variable that tells us why FMCS mediators tended to take more positive views of unions, was former union employment. In the study as a whole, the independent variables were agency affiliation and type of cases normally handled. Education, age, length of service as a mediator and prior work history proved to be the most important test variables, and the phenomena that we attempted to explain in Chapters 7 through 9 were the varying levels of job satisfaction between groups of mediators, beliefs concerning collective bargaining and attitudes toward professional issues, strategies and tactics.

The technique described in this example is three-variable cross tabulation. Such tabulations are valuable for determining whether people who share one characteristic (the independent variable) differ on others and hence form separate subgroups. Unfortunately, this technique can only be used where complete data sets are available, in this study for the 1985 results only. Thus the more elaborate analysis in the later chapters is limited to the results of the more recent survey, and a comparison between that and the earlier study could not be made.

APPENDIX B: THE 1985 SURVEY INSTRUMENT

Because the two questionnaires, the state and the FMCS versions, were almost identical, only the federal form is reproduced here. State mediators were also asked whether they devoted full- or part-time to agency work, and questions 106, 107 and 110 were omitted from the state form.

QUESTIONNAIRE

THE FEDERAL MEDIATOR

BACKGROUND AND CONCEPTION OF THE MEDIATION FUNCTION

Study By

Rutgers, The State University
Institute of Management and Labor Relations

In Cooperation With

Federal Mediation and Conciliation Service

Please return to:

Industrial Relations and Human Resources Department
Institute of Management and Labor Relations
Rutgers, The State University
New Brunswick, New Jersey 08903

FEDERAL MEDIATORS

The way people feel and the ideas they have differ because of differences in their backgrounds. We will use this background information to combine your answers by groups and to study the relationships between attitudes and personal characteristics.

Now for the background questions.

1. In which of the following areas do you work?

_____ (1) Eastern
_____ (2) Southern
_____ (3) Central
_____ (4) Western
_____ (5) National Office

2. What is your marital status?

_____ (1) single
_____ (2) married
_____ (3) widow or widower
_____ (4) divorced or separated

3. For how many children do you provide more than half the support?

    _____ (0) not married, or none
    _____ (1) one
    _____ (2) two
    _____ (3) three
    _____ (4) four
    _____ (5) five or more

4. What is your sex?

    _____ (1) male   _____ (2) female

5. How old were you at your last birthday?

    _____ (1) under 25 years old
    _____ (2) between 25 and 34
    _____ (3) between 35 and 44
    _____ (4) between 45 and 54
    _____ (5) between 55 and 64
    _____ (6) 65 or over

6. How much education have you had? (Check highest category completed.)

    _____ (1) did not complete high school
    _____ (2) completed high school
    _____ (3) some college
    _____ (4) completed college
    _____ (5) some graduate courses
    _____ (6) graduate degree(s) completed

7. How long have you been a mediator with this agency?

_____ (1) less than 1 year
_____ (2) 1 to 3 years
_____ (3) 4 to 6 years
_____ (4) 7 to 9 years
_____ (5) 10 to 12 years
_____ (6) 13 to 15 years
_____ (7) 16 to 18 years
_____ (8) 19 to 21 years
_____ (9) 22 or more years

8-9. Which of the following are included in your major work history? (Check all that are relevant.)

_____ (1) labor relations position(s) in industry
_____ (2) other supervisory or managerial position(s)
_____ (3) paid union position
_____ (4) unpaid union position
_____ (5) high school, college, or university faculty teaching

Were the above:

_____ (6) full time
_____ (7) part time

Independent practice or enterprise:

    (8) law
    (9) arbitration or other neutral labor relations enterprise
   (10) labor relations counseling to industry
   (11) labor relations counseling to labor unions

Other government neutral agency:

   (12) in labor relations field (NLRB, FLRC, etc.)

        specify _____

   (13) other
   (14) other work history not listed above

        specify _____

10. How long have you had experience as a labor-management mediator in
    this and other agencies?

    (0) less than 1 year
    (1) 1 to 3 years
    (2) 4 to 6 years
    (3) 7 to 9 years
    (4) 10 to 12 years
    (5) 13 to 15 years
    (6) 16 to 18 years
    (7) 19 to 21 years
    (8) 22 to 24 years
    (9) 25 years or more

11. During your work life, have you been a union member?

    ____ (0) at no time
    ____ (1) for less than 3 years
    ____ (2) from 3 to 6 years
    ____ (3) from 7 to 10 years
    ____ (4) 11 years or more

12. Which of the following best describes your parents or guardians main occupations?

    ____ (1) farmer or farm manager
    ____ (2) unskilled worker
    ____ (3) semi-skilled worker
    ____ (4) clerical worker
    ____ (5) sales worker
    ____ (6) skilled worker or foreman
    ____ (7) semi-professional or technical
    ____ (8) owner, manager, or official
    ____ (9) professional

13. How much education did your father have? (Check highest category completed.)

    ____ (1) some grammar school
    ____ (2) completed grammar school
    ____ (3) some high school
    ____ (4) completed high school

____ (5) some college
____ (6) completed college
____ (7) some graduate courses
____ (8) completed graduate degree(s)

14. At what annual salary are you currently employed?

____ (1) $25,000 - 29,999
____ (2) $30,000 - 34,999
____ (3) $35,000 - 39,999
____ (4) $40,000 - 44,999
____ (5) $45,000 - 49,999
____ (6) $50,000 - 54,999
____ (7) $55,000 - 59,999
____ (8) $60,000 - 64,999

15. How much is your total family income per year? Include income
    from all sources.

____ (1) $19,999 or less
____ (2) $20,000 - $29,999
____ (3) $30,000 - $39,999
____ (4) $40,000 - $49,999
____ (5) $50,000 - $59,999
____ (6) $60,000 - $69,999
____ (7) $70,000 - $79,999
____ (8) $80,000 - $89,999
____ (9) $90,000 - $99,999
____ (10) $100,000 or more

16. From what source or sources does your added family income come? (Check one or more.)

_____ (0) no added family income
_____ (1) spouse works
_____ (2) other occasional work
_____ (3) income from investments
_____ (4) other (specify) _____

17. Which of the following best describes your work situation?

_____ (1) I work full time as a mediator and have no supervisory or administrative duties.
_____ (2) I do mainly mediation work but have some supervisory or administrative duties.
_____ (3) I divide my time about evenly between mediation work and supervisory or administrative duties.
_____ (4) I perform mainly supervisory or administrative duties but do some mediation.
_____ (5) I work full time on supervisory or administrative duties and do no mediation.
_____ (6) Other (specify) _____

18. Which of the following best describes your case load?

_____ (1) all public sector
_____ (2) mostly public sector
_____ (3) mostly private sector
_____ (4) all private sector

19. In how many health care cases were you involved during the past year?

_____ (1) none
_____ (2) one
_____ (3) two
_____ (4) three - five
_____ (5) six - ten
_____ (6) over ten

20. List the organizations and associations in which you were a member during the past year (i.e., social, professional, fraternal, political organizations). If you were an elected or appointed officer, please indicate the position held.

_____

_____

_____

_____

_____

Now about your work as a mediator.

21. How much chance does your job give you to do the things you are best at?

    _____ (1) a very good chance
    _____ (2) a fairly good chance
    _____ (3) some chance
    _____ (4) very little chance
    _____ (5) no chance at all

22. About how much variety and change is there in your work?

    _____ (1) no variety and change
    _____ (2) very little variety and change
    _____ (3) some variety and change
    _____ (4) a great deal of variety and change

23. How well do you like meeting and mediating with the labor and management people you work with regularly?

    _____ (1) I like it very much.
    _____ (2) I like it fairly well.
    _____ (3) Sometimes I like it, and sometimes I dislike it.
    _____ (4) I dislike it somewhat.
    _____ (5) I dislike it very much.

24. How well do you like meeting and mediating with the labor and management people you work with from time to time?

_____ (1) I like it very much.
_____ (2) I like it fairly well.
_____ (3) Sometimes I like it, and sometimes I dislike it.
_____ (4) I dislike it somewhat.
_____ (5) I dislike it very much.

25. Looking at your present position and occupation realistically, what do you <u>expect</u> to be doing as a position or occupation five years from now?

_____ (1) same job
_____ (2) same job with increased income
_____ (3) move up in the same agency
_____ (4) move to another agency
_____ (5) retire
_____ (6) become an arbitrator
_____ (7) work for management
_____ (8) work for union
_____ (9) other. (specify) _____
_____

26. At what yearly income? _____

27. What is the prospect of your reaching this goal?

_____ (1) excellent
_____ (2) good
_____ (3) fair
_____ (4) poor
_____ (5) very poor

28. Considering your experience, education, and ability, what would you like to be doing as a position or occupation five years from now?

_____ (1) same job
_____ (2) same job with increased income
_____ (3) move up in the same agency
_____ (4) move to another agency
_____ (5) retire
_____ (6) become an arbitrator
_____ (7) work for management
_____ (8) work for a union
_____ (9) other (specify) _____

29. At what yearly income? _____

30. What is your prospect of reaching this goal?

_____ (1) excellent
_____ (2) good
_____ (3) fair
_____ (4) poor
_____ (5) very poor

31. How satisfied are you with your present salary?

_____ (1) completely satisfied
_____ (2) moderately satisfied
_____ (3) slightly satisfied
_____ (4) neither satisfied nor dissatisfied
_____ (5) slightly dissatisfied
_____ (6) Moderately dissatisfied
_____ (7) very dissatisfied

32. Considering your job as a whole, how well do you like it?

_____ (1) I don't like it at all.
_____ (2) I don't like it too well.
_____ (3) I like some things about it and dislike others.
_____ (4) I like it fairly well.
_____ (5) I like it very much.

33. Looking back over your career as realistically as possible, how well would you say you have done?

_____ (1) I have done much better than I expected.
_____ (2) I have done better than I expected.
_____ (3) I have done about as well as I expected.
_____ (4) I have not done as well as I expected.
_____ (5) I have not done at all as well as I expected.

34. What do you think is the most important reason for your answer to
#33? (Check all that apply)

      (1) The organization(s) have treated me generously.
      (2) The organization(s) have treated me fairly.
      (3) The organization(s) have treated me poorly.
      (4) I have done well on my own.
      (5) I have done fairly on my own.
      (6) I have done poorly on my own.
      (7) I have done well regardless of my educational background.
      (8) My education was an advantage.
      (9) I have done poorly regardless of my educational background.
      (10) Other (specify) _____

35. The quality of my education influenced my career

      (1) greatly.
      (2) somewhat.
      (3) a little.
      (4) not at all.

36. List below the last three jobs you had prior to coming to work for
this mediation agency. List the most recent job first, then the
next, and finally the least recent job. Also indicate the type of
organization (i.e., manufacturing, retail, etc.), the number of
employees, and your titles and duties.

Type of Organization	Number of Employees in Organization	Title and Duties

1. _____

2. _____

3. _____

The next sections deal with your opinions, beliefs, and attitudes. Please indicate your opinions on the line opposite each of the statements listed.

	Agree		Disagree	
Strongly	Mildly	Undecided	Mildly	Strongly

37. Unions must bear major responsibility for the inflation of the past ten years.

38. The negotiation of all labor-management contracts should be subject to compulsory arbitration.

	Agree Strongly/Mildly		Undecided	Disagree Mildly/Strongly	
	(1)	(2)	(3)	(4)	(5)
39. The rate of introduction of technological change should be determined by collective bargaining.					
40. Without a union to protect him/her, the average worker would be subject to the arbitrary decisions of management					
41. The free enterprise system today cannot operate without free collective bargaining.					
42. The mediator should serve the public's main interest which is to maintain productivity.					
43. The presence of a union makes it more difficult for the superior employee to get ahead on his/her own.					
44. All things considered, free collective bargaining has done a good job of adjusting the differences between management and labor.					

45. Unions should help industries in serious trouble by making wage and benefit concessions.

46. Unions may have been necessary at one time, but in general they have outlived their usefulness.

47. Collective bargaining has only been moderately successful in settling differences between large companies and large unions.

48. Although it has served a useful purpose in the past, collective bargaining is incapable of solving disputes growing out of job security issues.

49. Unions have seriously hindered attempts by American industries to meet productivity standards set by foreign industries.

Agree   Disagree
Strongly/Mildly   Undecided   Mildly/Strongly
(1)   (2)   (3)   (4)   (5)

50. The high standard of living in this country is due in large part to the activities of the labor movement.

51. In general, American management has come to accept the union's role in determining wages, hours, and working conditions.

52. The negotiation of labor-management contracts in the public sector should be subject to compulsory arbitration.

53. The negotiation of labor-management contracts in the health care industries should be subject to compulsory arbitration.

Below, please check one in each pair of alternatives:

54. The kind of job I would most prefer would be:

____ (1) a job where I am almost always on my own
____ (2) a job where there is nearly always someone available to help me
         with problems I don't know how to handle

____ (1) a job where I have to make many decisions by myself
____ (2) a job where I have to make few decisions by myself

____ (1) a job where my instructions are quite detailed and specific
____ (2) a job where my instructions are very general

____ (1) a job where I am the final authority on my work
____ (2) a job where there is nearly always a person or procedure that
         will catch my mistakes

____ (1) a job where I can be either highly successful or a complete
         failure
____ (2) a job where I can never be too successful but neither can I
         be a complete failure

____ (1) a job that is changing very little
____ (2) a job that is changing constantly

____ (1) an exciting job but one which might be done away with in a
         short time
____ (2) a less exciting job but one which undoubtedly would continue to
         exist for a long time

____ (1) a job where I am certain of my ability to perform well
____ (2) a job where I usually am pressed to the limit of my abilities

Some people are bothered more by certain kinds of things about their work and their jobs, while some people are bothered more by other kinds of things. How much are you bothered by the things listed below? (Check one alternative on each line.)

	Rarely or never bothered by it	Sometimes bothered by it	Frequently bothered by it
55. Feeling that I have too little authority to carry out responsibilities assigned to me.			
56. Being unclear on just what the scope and responsibilities of my job are.			
57. Feeling that too much responsibility and authority are delegated to me.			
58. Being unclear on what opportunities for promotion and advancement exist for me.			
59. Feeling that I have too heavy a work load.			
60. Thinking that I will not be able to satisfy the conflicting demands of the mediation situation.			
61. Feeling that I am not fully qualified to handle my job.			

62. Thinking that someone else may get the job above me that I am directly in line for.

63. Not knowing what my supervisor thinks of me, how he/she evaluates my performance.

64. The extent to which I can influence my immediate supervisor's actions and decisions that affect me.

65. The fact that I can't get information needed to carry out my job properly.

66. Feeling that my progress on the job is not what it should or could be.

67. Having to make decisions that affect the lives of individuals involved in negotiations with whom I have become acquainted.

68. My reporting requirements are excessive.

69. I am furnished inadequate informational and self-improvement materials.

About mediators and mediation:

70. When is the best time for a mediator to enter a labor-management situation?

    (1) at the start of negotiations
    (2) early in negotiations
    (3) when negotiations are well underway
    (4) at an impasse
    (5) after a strike has begun

71. Thinking back over the cases you have been involved with during the past few years, indicate roughly the percentage of cases which you have actively entered into: (Answer all)

	Percent
(1) at the start of negotiations	_____
(2) early in negotiations	_____
(3) when negotiations are well underway	_____
(4) at an impasse	_____
(5) after a strike has begun.	_____
	100%

72. The following are a set of possible ways of influencing the parties to a dispute to come to a mutually acceptable agreement. Please read all five. Then number them according to which you consider the most effective.

Place number "1" on the line next to the statement which best describes the method you consider most effective, place number "2" next to the statement which describes the method you consider the second most effective, and so on, placing a "5" next to the statement which describes the method you consider least effective or not at all effective.

_____ Showing both parties I am boss and forcing them to come to an agreement.

_____ Depending on my position as a mediator and representative of the public to influence both sides.

_____ Being friendly to both sides and trying to develop an atmosphere of agreement and mutual consent.

_____ Depending on my own ability as an expert in this kind of negotiating situation.

_____ Pointing out the benefits to both sides of settling their differences without the cost of a strike or lockout.

Once again, please indicate your opinion on the line opposite each of the following statements.

	Agree Strongly/Mildly		Undecided	Disagree Mildly/Strongly	
	(1)	(2)	(3)	(4)	(5)
73. Mediation is an art that has to be learned though experience.					
74. When meeting separately with one of the parties, it is quite in order for a mediator to support vigorously the position of the other party on an important issue.					
75. A mediator should be allowed to enter a labor dispute regardless of the wishes of the parties.					
76. In some cases the mediator may be required to deflate the parties' extreme positions.					
77. The mediator should clear in advance with each party before making suggestions at a joint negotiating session.					

78. Legislation should require the parties to utilize mediation before a strike can legally begin.

79. By and large, the American public does not appreciate the contribution of the mediator to the collective bargaining process.

80. Successful mediation depends more on the attitudes of the parties to a dispute than on the ability of the mediator.

81. Mediation is generally accepted among management people.

82. Union representatives, by and large, are willing to accept the service of mediators.

	Agree Strongly/Mildly (1)	(2)	Undecided (3)	Disagree Mildly/Strongly (4)	(5)
83. The possibility of recourse to such other dispute settlement procedures as interest arbitration or the Federal Service Impasse Panel has made mediation less effective in the public sector than in the private sector.					
84. Without mediation the number of strikes in industry would increase significantly.					
85. The continued effectiveness of a mediator depends upon not intruding when or where he/she is not wanted.					
86. The possibility of a strike provides the necessary atmosphere for the reconciliation of the parties' views.					
87. Requesting services of a mediator before a bona fide deadlock is often a trick used by a party to avoid its obligation to negotiate seriously.					

88. The need for mediation is a sign of immaturity on the part of management and labor.

89. The mediator's prime function is to represent the public's interest rather than to serve the parties.

90. Under some circumstances a mediator should make public his/her recommendations for the settlement of a dispute.

91. An occasional strike is useful in "clearing the air" in a collective bargaining dispute.

92. Except in rare cases, a mediator should not enter a dispute without the consent of both parties.

	Agree Strongly/Mildly		Undecided	Disagree Mildly/Strongly	
	(1)	(2)	(3)	(4)	(5)

93. When a mediator conveys a position from one party to another, he/she must exert the same degree of pressure that the parties would exert on each other if they were face-to-face.

94. The best way to exploit pressure in negotiations is to have the parties exert it face-to-face.

95. The mediator should never call for a separation of the parties unless there is a real possibility of achieving something.

96. Sometimes in joint conferences the mediator should aggressively support the position of one side or the other on an important issue.

97. Successful collective bargaining requires the pressure of contract expiration on the parties. Negotiations begun long before expiration of the agreement may solve some minor issues but will not settle major differences between the parties.

98. Dual mediation (mediators from more than one agency) is not satisfactory from the mediator's point of view.

99. Mediators should specialize by industry rather than being "general practitioners."

100. In important cases, the same mediator normally should be assigned to the same case the next time.

	Agree Strongly/Mildly (1)	(2)	Undecided (3)	Disagree Mildly/Strongly (4)	(5)
101. From the parties' points of view, dual mediation (mediators from more than one agency) provides better results than does solo mediation.					
102. Even in difficult cases, outside labor relations experts who are not full-time mediators do not contribute much to successful mediation.					
103. Laws forbidding strikes and lockouts in the public sector have made it more difficult for the mediator to help the parties reach an agreement.					
104. Panels should never be set up except on the recommendation of the initial mediator.					
105. Establishing a panel by adding one or more mediators on a case tends to depreciate the status of the initial mediator.					

105. Establishing a panel by adding one or more mediators on a case tends to depreciate the status of the initial mediator.

106. Regional Directors and Assistants should never participate in joint bargaining sessions.

107. National Office staff or representatives can at times be helpful in resolving difficult disputes by active participation.

108. If the site of bargaining moves, the initial mediator should always follow the case, regardless of distance.

109. If the mediator is given information by one party, he/she has no right to withhold it from the other party.

	Agree Strongly/Mildly		Undecided	Disagree Mildly/Strongly	
	(1)	(2)	(3)	(4)	(5)
110. When a National Office representative is working with a field mediator on a case, the former should always act as chairman of the Panel.					
111. A mediator's notion of what is equitable should never interfere with the primary objective, which is to settle a labor dispute.					
112. It is better for a mediator to be too forceful than too timid.					
113. There is no good way to measure the ability of a mediator.					
114. A majority of disputes involving mediation would turn out about the same without the participation of the mediator.					

115. The mediator is responsible for seeing that the
settlement does not violate
statutes or executive
guidelines.

116. Management's right to subcontract work should not
be limited by the collec-
tive bargaining agreement.

117. Management's right to re-
locate a plant should not
be subject to collective
bargaining.

118. Prior to collective bargaining, management should
be required to provide the
union with any relevant
financial data it requests.

119. Public sector bargaining
frequently is complicated
by the mediator's inability
to discover who or which
group has the ultimate
decision-making power.

120. Did you participate in the 1964 survey?

     _____ (1) yes

     _____ (2) no

We would appreciate your comments on anything which we have failed to cover in the questionnaire but which you feel is an important element in your work situation.

BIBLIOGRAPHY

General Studies and Monographs

Bellush, Jewel and Bernard. _Union Power and New York: Victor Gotbaum and District Council 37_. New York: Praeger, 1984.

Douglas, Ann. _Industrial Peacemaking_. New York: Columbia University Press, 1962.

Dulles, Rhea Foster and Melvyn Dubofsky. _Labor in America, A History_. 4th ed. Arlington Heights, Ill.: Harlan Davidson, Inc., 1984.

Fisher, Roger and William Ury with Bruce Patton, eds. _Getting to Yes: Negotiating Agreement Without Giving In_. Boston: Houghton Mifflin Co., 1981.

Indik, Bernard P., Bernard Goldstein, Jack Chernick and Monroe Berkowitz. _The Mediator: Background, Self-Image, and Attitudes_. New Brunswick, N.J.: Institute of Management and Labor Relations, Rutgers, The State University, 1966.

Jackson, Elmore. _Meeting of Minds: A Way to Peace Through Mediation_. New York: McGraw-Hill, Inc., 1952.

Kochan, Thomas A. _Collective Bargaining and Industrial Relations: From Theory to Policy and Practice_. Homewood, Ill.: Richard D. Irwin, Inc., 1980.

Kolb, Deborah. _The Mediators_. Cambridge, Mass.: Massachusetts Institute of Technology Press, 1983.

Kressel, Kenneth. _Labor Mediation: An Exploratory Survey_. Albany, N.Y.: Association of Labor Mediation Agencies, 1972.

Lester, Richard A. _Labor Arbitration in State and Local Government: An Examination of Experience in Eight States and New York City_. Princeton,

N.J.: Industrial Relations Section, Department
of Economics, Princeton University, 1984.

Lieberman, Myron. Public-Sector Bargaining: A
Policy Reappraisal. Lenox, Mass.: D.C. Heath &
Co., 1980.

Maggiolo, Walter A. Techniques of Mediation in
Labor Disputes. Dobbs Ferry, N.Y.: Oceana
Press, 1971.

Millis, Harry A. and Emily Clark Brown. From the
Wagner Act to Taft-Hartley: A Study of National
Labor Policy and Labor Relations. Chicago:
University of Chicago Press, 1950.

Oberer, Walter E., Kurt L. Hanslowe and Jerry R.
Andersen. Cases and Materials on Labor Law:
Collective Bargaining in a Free Society.
American Casebook Series. 2nd ed. St. Paul,
Minn.: West Publishing Co., 1979.

Peters, Edward. Conciliation in Action: Principles and Techniques. New London, Conn.: National Foremen's Institute, 1952.

Robins, Eva and Tia Schneider Denenberg. A Guide
for Labor Mediators. Honolulu: Industrial Relations Center, College of Business Administration, University of Hawaii, 1976.

Simkin, William E. Mediation and the Dynamics
of Collective Bargaining. Washington, D.C.:
Bureau of National Affairs, 1971.

_____ and Nicholas A. Fidandis. Mediation and
the Dynamics of Collective Bargaining. 2nd ed.
Washington, D.C.: Bureau of National Affairs,
1986.

Spencer, W. H. The National Railroad Adjustment
Board. Chicago: The University of Chicago
Press, 1938.

Stern, James L., Charles M. Rehmus, J. Joseph
Lowenberg, Hirschel Kasper and Barbara Dennis.
Final-Offer Arbitration. Lexington, Mass.:
Lexington Books, 1975.

Weinberg, William M. "An Administrative History
    of the New Jersey State Board of Mediation."
    Ph.D. dissertation, University of Pennsylvania,
    1964.

Weisenfeld, Allan. <u>Mediation and the Development
    of Industrial Relations in New Jersey</u>. Newark,
    N.J.: New Jersey State Board of Mediation,
    1966.

Witte, Edwin. <u>Historical Survey of Labor Arbi-
    tration</u>. Philadelphia, Pa.: University of
    Pennsylvania Press, 1952.

Zack, Arnold M. <u>Public Sector Mediation</u>. Wash-
    ington, D.C.: Bureau of National Affairs, Inc.,
    1985.

<u>Conference Proceedings and Collected Works</u>

Association of Labor Relations Agencies. <u>New
    Techniques in Labor Dispute Resolution. A Re-
    port of the Twenty-Third Conference of the
    Association of Labor Mediation Agencies (July
    28-August 2, 1974) and the Second Conference of
    the Society of Professionals in Dispute Resolu-
    tion, November 11-13, 1974</u>. Washington, D.C.:
    Bureau of National Affairs, 1976.

_____. "New Vistas in Mediation. Proceedings
    of the Fourth Conference, Association of State
    Mediation Agencies, Ithaca, New York, June 27-
    29, 1955." <u>Labor Law Journal</u> 6 (1955): 587-601.

_____. "Selected Proceedings of the 32nd
    Annual Conference of the Association of Labor
    Relations Agencies."(July 17-22, 1983, Moncton,
    New Brunswick.) Offset, n.p., n.d.

_____. <u>Selected Proceedings of the Twenty-
    Fifth Annual Conference of the Association of
    Labor Mediation Agencies (August 14-20, 1976)
    Ottawa, Canada</u>. N.p., ALMA, n.d.

Industrial Relations Research Association. <u>Pro-
    ceedings of the Thirty-Seventh Annual Meeting,
    December 28-30, 1984, Dallas, Texas</u>. Madison,
    Wisc.: IRRA, 1985.

New York State Public Employment Relations Bureau
    and New York State School of Industrial and La-
    bor Relations at Cornell. "Symposium on Police
    and Firefighter Arbitration in New York State,
    December 1-3, 1976, Albany, New York." Offset,
    n.p., 1977.

Public Employment Relations Service. Portrait of
    a Process: Collective Negotiations in Public
    Employment. Fort Washington, Pa.: Labor Rela-
    tions Press, 1979.

Rehmus, Charles M., ed. The Railway Labor Act at
    Fifty. Washington, D.C.: United States
    Government Printing Office, 1976.

Society of Professionals in Dispute Resolution.
    Bringing the Dispute Resolution Community
    Together, 1985 Proceedings, 13th International
    Conference, October 27-30, 1985, Boston, Massa-
    chusetts. Washington, D.C.: SPIDR, 1986.

_____. Creative Approaches to Dispute Reso-
    lution, 1982 Proceedings, Tenth Annual Confer-
    ence, October 17-19, 1982, Detroit, Michigan.
    N.p., SPIDR, 1983.

_____. Dispute Resolution: Public Policy and
    the Practitioner, 1977 Proceedings, Fifth
    Annual Meeting, October 23-26, 1977. N.p.,
    SPIDR, 1978.

_____. Neutrals' Response to a Society in
    Dispute: A Multi-Track Conference on Dispute
    Resolution, 1980 Proceedings, Eighth Annual
    Meeting, October 19-22, 1980. Washington,
    D.C.: SPIDR, 1981.

_____. The Public Interest and the Role of
    the Neutral in Dispute Settlement, Proceedings
    of the Inaugural Convention of the Society of
    Professionals in Dispute Resolution, Reston,
    Virginia, October 17-19, 1973. Albany, N.Y.:
    The Society, 1974.

Zack, Arnold and William M. Weinberg. Resource
    Manual for Impasse Procedures in Public School
    Negotiations. New Brunswick, N.J.: Rutgers,
    Institute of Management and Labor Relations,
    1976.

Zagora, Sam, ed., <u>Public Workers and Public
    Unions</u>. Englewood Cliffs, N.J.: Prentice-Hall,
    1972.

Articles

Anderson, Arvid and Joan Weitzman. "The Scope of
    Bargaining in the Public Sector." <u>Portrait of
    a Process: Collective Negotiations in Public
    Employment</u>, Public Employment Relations Ser-
    vices, pp. 173-95. Fort Washington, Pa.: Labor
    Relations Press, 1979.

Ashenfelder, Orley and David Bloom. "Why Are
    Union Offers Selected Most of the Time in
    Final-Offer Arbitration?" Working Paper No.
    160, presented at the Annual Spring Meeting,
    IRRA, Hawaii, March 16-18, 1983.

Barrett, Jerome T. "The Psychology of a Media-
    tor." Occasional Paper No. 83-1, March 1983,
    Society of Professionals in Dispute Resolu-
    tion, Committee on Research and Education.
    Washington, D.C.: SPIDR, 1983.

Berkowitz, Monroe, Bernard Goldstein and Bernard
    P. Indik, "The State Mediator: Background,
    Self-Image, and Attitudes." <u>Industrial and
    Labor Relations Review</u> 17 (1964): 257-75.

Bloom, David E. "Customized 'Final-Offer': New
    Jersey's Arbitration Law." <u>Monthly Labor
    Review</u>, September 1980, pp. 30-33.

Colosi, Thomas. "Negotiation and Dispute Resolu-
    tion: A Process Perspective," in <u>Creative
    Approaches to Dispute Resolution, 1982 Pro-
    ceedings, Tenth Annual Conference, October
    17-19, 1982, Detroit, Michigan</u>, Society of
    Professionals in Dispute Resolution. N.p.:
    SPIDR, 1983.

D'Alba, Joel A. "The Nature of the Duty to
    Bargain in Good Faith," in <u>Portrait of a Pro-
    cess: Collective Negotiations in Public Em-
    ployment</u>, Public Employment Relations Ser-
    vices, pp. 149-172. Fort Washington, Pa.:
    Labor Relations Press, 1979.

Douglas, Ann. "What Can Research Tell Us About
    Mediation?" Labor Law Journal 6 (1955):
    545-52.

Fishgold, Herbert. "Dispute Resolution in the
    Public Sector: The Role of the Federal Media-
    tion and Conciliation Service." Labor Law
    Journal 28 (1976): 731-37.

Freilicher, Frederic. Standards of Admission
    to Membership in a Professional Organization
    of Neutrals in Labor Relations. N.p., Asso-
    ciation of Labor Relations Agencies, 1972.

Friedman, David R. and Stuart S. Mukamal. "Wis-
    consin's Mediation-Arbitration Law: What Has it
    Done to Bargaining?" Journal of Collective
    Negotiations in the Public Sector 13 (1984):
    171-89.

Gershenfeld, Walter J. "Public Employee Union-
    ization -- An Overview," in Portrait of a Pro-
    cess: Collective Negotiations in Public Em-
    ployment, Public Employment Relations Ser-
    vices, pp. 3-27. Fort Washington, Pa.: Labor
    Relations Press, 1979.

Gordon, Michael E. and Aaron J. Nurick. "Psycho-
    logical Approaches to the Study of Unions and
    Union-Management Relations." Psychological
    Bulletin 90 (1981): 293-306.

Hartfield, Edward P. "Becoming a Mediator," in
    Creative Approaches to Dispute Resolution, 1982
    Proceedings, Tenth Annual Conference, October
    17-19, 1982, Detroit, Michigan, Society of
    Professionals in Dispute Resolution. Washing-
    ton, D.C.: SPIDR, 1983.

Hogler, Raymond and Curt Krikscium. "Impasse
    Resolution in Public Sector Collective Negotia-
    tions: A Proposed Procedure." Industrial Re-
    lations Law Journal 6 (1984): 481-510.

Kochan, Thomas A. "U.S. Industrial Relations Sys-
    tem in Transition: A Summary Report," in Pro-
    ceedings of the Thirty-Seventh Annual Meeting,
    December 28-30, 1984, Dallas, Texas, Industrial
    Relations Research Association, pp. 261-76.
    Madison. Wisc.: IRRA, 1985.

Landsberger, Henry A. "The Behavior and Person-
    ality of the Labor Mediator: The Parties' Per-
    ception of Mediator Behavior." Personnel Psy-
    chology 13 (1960): 501-508.

_____. "Final Report on a Research Project in
    Mediation." Labor Law Journal 7 (1956): 501-
    508.

_____. "Interaction Process Analysis of the
    Mediation of Labor Management Disputes."
    Journal of Abnormal Social Psychology 51
    (1955): 552-58.

_____. "Interim Report of a Research Pro-
    ject on Mediation." Labor Law Journal (1955):
    552-60.

MacKranz, James. "General Role of Mediation in
    Collective Bargaining." Labor Law Journal 11
    (1960): 453-60.

Manson, Julius. "Mediators as Arbitrators."
    Labor Law Journal 6 (1955) 587-601.

McMurray, Kay. "The Federal Mediation and
    Conciliation Service: Serving Labor-Management
    Relations in the Eighties." Labor Law Journal
    34 (1983): 67-71.

Northrup, Herbert R. "Mediation -- the Viewpoint
    of the Mediated." Labor Law Journal 13 (1962):
    67-71.

Peters, Edward. "The Mediator: A Neutral, a Cata-
    lyst, or a Leader." Labor Law Journal 9
    (1958): 765-69.

Rehmus, Charles M. "Mediation and Conciliation."
    Labor Law Journal 4 (1953): 141-43.

_____. "The Mediation of Industrial Conflict:
    A Note on the Literature." Journal of Conflict
    Resolution 9 (1965): 18-26.

Ross, Jerome H. "Federal Mediation in Public Ser-
    vice." Monthly Labor Review, February 1976,
    pp. 41-45.

Schuck, Joseph P. "History of Dispute Resolu-
    tion," in Selected Proceedings of the Twenty-
    Fifth Annual Conference of the Association of
    Labor Mediation Agencies (August 15-20, 1976)
    Ottawa, Canada, Association of Labor Relations
    Agencies, pp. 95-109. N.p., ALMA, n.d.

Shaw, Lee C. "The Development of State and
    Federal Laws," in Public Workers and Public
    Unions, edited by Sam Zagoria, pp. 20-36.
    Englewood Cliffs, N.J.: Prentice-Hall, 1972.

Stutz, Robert L. "Troikas, Duets and Prima Donnas
    in Labor Mediation." Labor Law Journal 13
    (1962): 845-52.

Stulberg, Joseph B. "A Mediator's Neutrality:
    Fact or Fiction?" in Creative Approaches to
    Dispute Resolution, 1982 Proceedings, Tenth
    Annual Conference, October 17-19, 1982, De-
    troit, Michigan, Society of Professionals in
    Dispute Resolution. Washington, D.C.: SPIDR,
    1983.

Tener, Jeffrey B. "Mediator Skills," in Creative
    Approaches to Dispute Resolution, 1982 Pro-
    ceedings, Tenth Annual Conference, October 17-
    19, 1982, Detroit, Michigan, Society of Pro-
    fessionals in Dispute Resolution. Washington,
    D.C.: SPIDR, 1983.

Wasserman, Don S. "A Union View of the Neutral,"
    in Creative Approaches to Dispute Resolution,
    1982 Proceedings, Tenth Annual Conference,
    October 17-19, 1982, Detroit, Michigan, So-
    ciety of Professionals in Dispute Resolution.
    Washington, D.C.: SPIDR, 1983.

Weinberg, William M. "Bureaucratic Expediency and
    the Ethics of Mediation." Presented to the
    Association of Labor Mediation Agencies, August
    15, 1967, and condensed in Labor Relations
    Yearbook, 1967, Bureau of National Affairs,
    pp. 159-63. Washington, D.C.: BNA, 1968, and
    Labor Relations Reporter 65 LRR 338.

_____. "Ethical Questions Confronting the
    Mediator," in Dispute Resolution: Public Pol-
    icy and the Practitioner, 1977 Proceedings,
    Fifth Annual Meeting, October 23-26, 1977,

Society of Professionals in Dispute Resolution,
pp. 96-107. Washington, D.C.: SPIDR, 1978.

_____. "Impasse Procedures," in <u>Resource
Manual for Impasse Procedures in Public School
Negotiations</u>, edited by Arnold Zack and William
M. Weinberg. New Brunswick, N.J.: Rutgers In-
stitute of Management and Labor Relations,
1976.

_____. "Mediators: 25 Years Ago and Today," in
<u>Bringing the Dispute Resolution Community
Together, 1985 Proceedings, 13th International
Conference, October 27-30, 1985, Boston, Massa-
chusetts</u>, Society of Professionals in Dispute
Resolution, pp. 75-85. Washington, D.C.:
SPIDR, 1986.

Weisenfeld, Allan. "Profile of a Labor Mediator."
<u>Labor Law Journal</u> 13 (1962): 864-73.

Yager, Paul. "Mediation: A Conflict Resolution
Technique in the Industrial Community and Public Sectors," in <u>New Techniques in Labor
Dispute Resolution. A Report of the Twenty-
Third Conference of the Association of Labor
Mediation Agencies (July 28-August 2, 1974) and
the Second Conference of the Society of Professionals in Dispute Resolution, November 11-
13, 1974</u>, Association of Labor Relations
Agencies, pp. 122-30. Washington, D.C.: Bureau
of National Affairs, 1976.

Zack, Arnold M. "Impasses, Strikes and Resolutions," in <u>Public Workers and Public Unions</u>,
edited by Sam Zagoria, pp. 101-21. Englewood
Cliffs, N.J.: Prentice-Hall, 1972.

INDEX

A

AFSCME (see American Federation of State, County and Municipal Employees)
age 27, 30, 35-36, 37, 46, 103-104, 105-107, 112, 132, 134, 144
agency affiliation 62, 66, 109-110, 115, 117, 119, 122-25, 135, 138, 144
ALMA (see Association of Labor Mediation Agencies)
ALRA (see Association of Labor Relations Agencies)
American Federation of Labor (AFL) 9, 13
American Federation of Labor-Congress of Industrial Organizations (AFL-CIO) 56
American Federation of State, County and Municipal Employees (AFSCME) 25, 80
American Telegraph and Telephone 56
Americans Against Union Control of Government 26
arbitration 62, 127
    binding 77, 95
    compulsory 77-78, 82, 95, 119, 127, 136
    interest 76-78, 125
Arkansas 6
ASMA (see Association of State Mediation Agencies)
Association of Labor Mediation Agencies (ALMA) 3, 16
Association of Labor Relations Agencies (ALRA) vii, 1, 5, 6, 16, 24-25, 26, 38, 132, 141
Association of State Mediation Agencies (ASMA) 1, 15-16

B

Barrett, Jerome T. 55
Berkowitz, Monroe 133
boards of inquiry 79, 83
Bureau of Labor Statistics 25

C

Canada 1, 5, 6, 52
career
    goals 50
    plans 45-46, 54, 105-107, 113, 133-34
    satisfaction 44-45, 105, 112-13, 133-34
Carter, James 20
civil service 5
Civil Service Reform Act of 1978 18-19

collective bargaining
  academic 18, 25
  attitudes toward 56, 62
  health care industry 4, 18, 21, 72, 75, 78, 83,
    97, 119, 120, 127
  police and fire 78, 82, 120
  private sector 70, 71, 75, 88
  professional workers 18
  public health and safety 120, 136
  public sector 3, 4, 7, 18, 19-20, 21, 25, 56,
    57, 65, 70, 71, 72, 75-76, 78, 81, 82, 88,
    97, 111, 119, 120, 124, 125, 135, 136, 138
  scope of 62, 63-64, 65, 66, 114, 136
  service industry 18, 21
confidentiality 92
Congress of Industrial Organizations (CIO) 13
Connecticut 98
Cooper Union 18
Cornell School of Industrial and Labor Relations 1
Consumer Price Index 42
Cramer's V 143
cross tabulations 142-43
  three variable 144

D

demographic characteristics 27, 132, 141
descriptive statistics 141
Douglas, Ann 1
duty to bargain 64, 66

E

economic environment 63, 66, 95, 136, 138
economic issues 59-60
education 27, 28, 29-30, 31-32, 37, 40, 42, 45-46,
  66, 67, 103-107, 111-12, 114, 115, 117, 119,
  120, 124, 126, 127, 130, 133, 134, 135, 137,
  138, 139, 144
  attitude toward 45
employer, attitude toward 45
employment
  past 29, 32, 37-38, 40, 63-64, 66, 105, 108,
    109, 111-12, 115, 117, 119, 120, 123, 124,
    125, 128, 130, 144
  public sector 112, 128
environment, influence of (see also economic
  environment) 132, 138-39
equity 72, 111
Erdman Act 10
Executive Order 10988 18

Executive Order 11491   18-19
explanatory variable   143-44

F

fact-finding   62, 76, 77, 78, 95, 125
Fair Labor Standards Act   20
Federal Mediation and Conciliation Service (FMCS)
        vii, 2, 3, 4, 5, 14, 15, 16, 20-21, 22, 26,
        38, 40-41, 52, 55, 83, 89, 131, 134
    differences among regions   6, 31-32, 33-34, 39,
        41, 43, 44, 51-53, 54, 55, 59, 63, 66, 69-70,
        84, 86, 88, 92, 96, 132, 134, 136, 137, 139,
        140
    jurisdiction over public sector cases   80
    reorganization   26, 85
Fibreboard Paper Products Co. v. NLRB   64, 65
Fishgold, Herbert   19
Florida   42
FMCS (see Federal Mediation and Conciliation
        Service)
frequency distributions   141-42

G

gender   35, 41
General Electric v. NLRB   64
General Motors   56
Gershenfeld, Walter J.   81, 97
Gilbert, Jacob H.   25
Government Accounting Office   20

H

Hartfield, Edward P.   41, 55
Haymarket Riot   9
health care workers   21

I

Illinois   9, 42
IMLR (see Rutgers Institute of Management and Labor
        Relations)
income   28-29, 33-34
independent variable   144
Indik, Bernard P.   55
Industrial Relations Research Association (IRRA)
        15, 16, 24, 38
IRRA (see Industrial Relations Research Associa-
        tion)

J

job
   satisfaction   43-45, 53, 54, 100-101, 133, 134,
      142, 144
      factors in   46-50, 53, 101-103, 112-13,
      134-35, 142
   security   52
   stress   50-52, 55, 134
jurisdiction of agencies   70

K

Kennedy, John F.   18
Kochan, Thomas A.   81, 90, 98, 99
Kolb, Deborah   55, 67, 70, 89, 97, 99, 115, 121,
      130, 140

L

labor force   21, 24
Landrum-Griffith Act   15, 25
Landsberger, Henry   1, 8
length of service   28, 36, 101, 105, 107, 111, 112,
      115-17, 119, 120, 121, 122, 125, 126, 127,
      128, 130, 132, 133, 134-35, 137, 138, 139,
      140, 144
level of significance   143

M

management experience   27, 29, 38, 64, 65, 78, 137
management prerogatives   62-66, 108, 110, 114, 136
marital status   27, 30, 35, 40, 132
Maryland   9
Massachusetts   9
McMurray, Kay   4, 21, 70
mediation
   ad hoc   87-89, 97, 137
   dual   88-89, 97, 117, 127, 137
   experience (see employment, past)
   mandatory   74, 76, 95, 136
   panel   87-89, 97, 117
   preventive   122, 124
   study of   1-3, 90, 97
mediators
   activism   2, 70-71, 88-90, 96, 121-22, 123, 127,
      128, 137, 140
   ad hoc   87
   appreciation of   84, 85, 95, 97
   influence on parties   69-70
   intervention   71

profile (see individual demographic characteris-
    tics)
recognition of 95, 115
relationship with clients 48-49, 53, 55, 85-86,
    95, 96, 100, 101-102, 104-105, 107, 112, 115-
    16, 127, 134, 135, 136-37
responsibility 71-73, 90, 111, 112, 113, 114,
    138
training 38, 85
Metzger, Norman 97

N
National Association of Manufacturers 13
National Education Association 20
National Industrial Recovery Act 11
National Labor Relations Act (NLRA) 11-12, 19, 25,
    137
    industrial relations system 15, 39, 56. 57, 60-
        61, 108, 135
    health care amendments to 18, 75, 83
National Labor Relations Board (NLRB) 12, 13, 18,
    25, 56, 64, 65, 66
National League of Cities v. Usery 20
National Mediation Board 10
New York 9
New York State Board of Mediation 10
Nixon, Richard M. 18-19
NLRA (see National Labor Relations Act)
NLRB (see National Labor Relations Board)
Norris-LaGuardia Act 11
North Carolina 6

O
Office of Naval Research 1
Ohio 9, 42

P
Pennsylvania 9
Pennsylvania Labor Relations Board 25
phi 143
plant relocation 62, 64, 114, 136
probability 141-142
productivity 72, 111, 113, 114, 135, 138
professionalism 37-39, 85, 139
public interest 111, 113, 114, 138
Public Service Research Council 20, 26
Puerto Rico 5, 6, 21

R

Railway Labor Board   10
Raskin, Abe   81
Reagan, Ronald   20
recruitment   29, 41, 42, 129, 135
residual   143
retirement plans   46, 54, 107, 134, 140
risk preference   48, 49, 51-52, 54, 55
Roosevelt, Franklin D.   13
Roybal, Edward R.   25
Rutgers Institute of Management and Labor Relations
    (IMLR)   vii, 1, 3, 27
Rutgers 1960s studies   vii, 1-4, 56, 97, 100, 128,
    132-33, 140

S

salary (see also income)   33, 35, 42, 46-47, 132,
    134
  expectations   45
  satisfaction   46-48, 103, 105, 107, 112, 134
School Boards Association   20
service workers   21
skill use   48, 53
Smith-Connally Act   13
social background   27, 30, 40, 132
Society of Professionals in Dispute Resolution
    (SPIDR)   16, 24, 38
specialization   87, 115, 117, 127, 130, 137
SPIDR (see Society of Professionals in Dispute
    Resolution)
statistics   141-44
strikes   62, 74, 81-82, 95, 124, 125
  threat of   75-76
Stulberg, Joseph B.   81
subcontracting   62, 64, 114
Supreme Court   18, 19, 20, 64
Susskind, Larry   81

T

tactics   91, 93-95, 96, 99, 121-22, 126-28, 130-31,
    137-38, 144
Taft-Hartley Act   14, 18, 70, 75
Taylor, George   82
technical assistance   99, 125, 130
Tener, Jeffery B.   vii, 71, 80
timing   92-93, 95-96, 99, 121, 122-26, 128, 130,
    137

type of cases handled   2, 33-35, 37-38, 42, 56, 57,
     60, 62, 66, 67, 78, 81, 89, 91, 96, 100, 101,
     104-105, 108-113, 114, 115, 117, 119-126,
     128, 130, 138-39, 144
type of duties   33, 132-33

                              U

unions   2, 18, 56, 115
   affiliation with   3, 24-25, 27, 40, 57-58, 65,
      67, 78, 109, 127
   attitudes toward   3, 20, 39, 57-61, 65, 108-11,
      113, 135, 138, 144
   employment by   3, 27, 29, 32, 35, 38, 57, 59,
      64, 109-110, 113, 120, 124, 138, 144
   public employee   18-20, 24, 76
United States Chamber of Commerce   13
United States Conciliation Service (USCS)   11, 12,
     13, 14
University of Pittsburgh   25
USCS (see United States Conciliation Service)
Usery, W. J.   19

                              V

variable   143-44
variety   48, 54
Vietnam War   3
Virgin Islands   21
voluntary organizations   42
   membership in   31, 41-42

                              W

Wagner Act   11-12, 75
War Labor Board   11, 13
Wasserman, Don S.   80
Weinberg, William M.   vii, 71
Wisconsin   19
Wollett, Donald H.   82

                             YZ

Yager, Paul   vii, 41
Yeshiva   18, 25
Zack, Arnold M.   67, 71, 80, 97, 130